PALMS & THORNS

SERMONS FOR LENT AND EASTER

CYCLE B
FIRST LESSON TEXTS

DONALD MACLEOD

C.S.S. Publishing Co., Inc.

Lima, Ohio

PALMS AND THORNS

Copyright © 1990 by
The C.S.S. Publishing Company, Inc.
Lima, Ohio

All rights reserved. No part of this publication may be reproduced, stored in a retrieval system, or transmitted in any form or by any means, electronic, mechanical, photocopying, recording, or otherwise, without the prior permission of the publisher. Inquiries should be addressed to: The C.S.S. Publishing Company, Inc., 628 South Main Street, Lima, Ohio 45804.

Library of Congress Cataloging-in-Publication Data
Macleod, Donald, 1914-
Palms and thorns / by Donald Macleod.
  p.   cm.
ISBN 1-55673-224-4 : $7.25
 1. Lenten sermons.   2. Holy-Week sermons.   3. Eastertide—Sermons.
 4. Sermons, American.   5. Bible. O.T.—Sermons.   6. Bible. NT.
Acts—Sermons.   I. Title.
BV4277.M22   1990
252'.62—dc20
                                                    90-42981
                                                         CIP

9054 / ISBN 1-55673-224-4   PRINTED IN U.S.A.

Contents

Lent

Ash Wednesday	Joel 2:12-19	Putting Lent into Focus	7
Lent 1	Genesis 9:8-17	Reclaiming Our Covenant	11
Lent 2	Genesis 17:1-10, 15-19	Rediscovering Our Spiritual Dimension	15
Lent 3	Exodus 20:1-17	Restoring Our Sense of Priorities	21
Lent 4	2 Chronicles 36:14-23	Reviving Our Moral Responsibility	27
Lent 5	Jeremiah 31:31-34	Returning to Genuine Religion	31
Passion Sunday	Isaiah 50:4-9a	Reconciling Palms and Thorns	37

Holy Week

Monday	Isaiah 42:1-9	Servants Without Fiber	43
Tuesday	Isaiah 49:1-6	Service Beset by "What's the Use?"	47
Wednesday	Isaiah 50:4-9a	Service Without Witness	53
Maundy Thursday	Psalm 116:12-19	Servant Worship	57
Good Friday	Isaiah 52:13—53:12	The Vicarious Servant	61

Easter

The Resurrection of Our Lord	Isaiah 25:6-9	The Outcome of Easter Faith	67
Easter 2	Acts 4:32-37	Beginning with Easter	71
Easter 3	Acts 3:13-19	Passing the Easter Miracle On	75
Easter 4	Acts 4:5-13	An Easter Dividend: Courage To Be and To Do	81
Easter 5	Acts 8:26-40	Easter Journeys Out and In	87
Easter 6	Acts 10:44-48	Easter Turns ONLY into ALSO	91
Easter 7	Acts 1:1-11	Ascension Day: A Perspective on Ascension	97
Easter 8	Acts 1:14-17, 21-26	Readying the Twelve for Mission	103

Putting Lent into Focus

Ash Wednesday   Joel 2:12-19

Within the lifetime of many of us of the Reformed or Free Church tradition, any serious observance of the season of Lent had been somewhat rare or, indeed, optional. Lent was the private and sophisticated preserve of the Episcopalians and Roman Catholics and of a few Protestants who wanted others to think they were "with it." Nowadays, however, the whole Christian world recognizes Lent almost routinely, and seemingly it has now a secure place with everyone in the Church Year.

Familiarity with Lent has bred, however, an unfortunate spirit of neglect due largely to a misunderstanding of its meaning and significance. In our era of quick fixes and fast everything, Lent as a season seems unduly long. One clergyperson has said, "My people just can't remain sorry for their sins for forty days." Some parishioners complain about clergy who seem to cram every available hour of Lent with homilies, prayer vigils, and silent reflections to such a degree that everyday living seems to be an intrusion.

Palms and Thorns

It would appear, then, that the mechanics of Lent have been put into the ascendancy, and hence the church needs now to get back to basics and teach laypersons what Lent is all about. This would involve mainly our getting rid of the many misunderstandings which people continue to foster; e.g., someone says, "I'm giving up cigarettes for Lent" or "Beer is off my list during Lent." The Lenten spirit is not a catalog of negatives! Or, what is equally off-beat: some preachers get the sequence of Lent all mixed up. They sing and preach about the Cross on Ash Wednesday and go on talking about it for forty days. Round and round in a circle they go and fail to instruct their people that Lent is a process, a going up from where we are to the Cross and to Easter Day. Lent begins with ourselves and our alienation from God through sin; it ends with the price of the Cross and the joy of eternal liberation at the Empty Tomb.

First of all, then, we can put Lent properly into focus by facing up to the reality of the human struggle. We are today the unconscious victims of moral and spiritual relativism. Our lifestyles reflect a philosophy of "anything goes." Ash Wednesday stops us "up short" and urges us to look and listen: look at ourselves, at our "is-ness," and listen to a call to "ought-ness," to a voice inside and beyond ourselves.

This is what the prophet Joel has to say to us today. His imagery and metaphors boggle our twentieth-century minds, but his Day of the Lord means simply that when moral rebellion goes too far, a time of judgment occurs and God says, "No further!" In the human struggle there comes a time when the "exceeding sinfulness of sin" brings its harvest upon us and people yearn for a way out. That way is God's way and through his prophets and apostles, his "errand runners," comes his call: Repent!

Here again, however, such a word needs clarification. Yes, it involves being sorry for our sins, but this is apt to

Lent and Easter

become merely a negative, closed-end experience. Truly, it must begin as Joel suggests, "Rend your heart and not your garments," (2:12 RSV) but this attitude of humility must accept the *discipline* of repentance, i.e., a Lenten call to serious and regular acts of worship and devotion. Billy Graham, for example, reads five Psalms every morning and, therefore, covers the Book every month. Could not each of us read through the four Gospels every week in Lent and select also one great saint and read his or her biography — a Livingstone, a Schweitzer, a Mother Teresa — and see in them what our poor nature can become?

Another thought: Lent must not become a season focused exclusively upon the individual. We need the comradeship of fellow Christians in our pilgrimage from recognition of our frailties to the level of victory. As someone once said: "The New Testament knows nothing of a solitary Christian." The ancient prophet speaks of this return to God, but never does he see it as a solitary venture of an individual doing his or her own devotional thing. His phrases are: "the solemn assembly," "the congregation," "the ministers of the Lord," and "my people." To be complete and genuine Lent must be a parish experience, a movement of the whole people of God in community, when together the church members put their spiritual responsibility into right perspective.

And now: What of it all? Or, as a philosopher used to ask: "Where is the hanging up place of the chain?" Or, to use a modern cliche: "Is there light at the end of the tunnel?" The end is positive, but it hangs upon the tremendous word "if." If Joel's people "return to the Lord"; if their worship is genuine and reflects spiritual depth — then God will fulfill his promises which are for the nation's good. He will give his Spirit to them and out of the reality of this relationship will come the instruments of their salvation. (2:28 RSV) If,

Palms and Thorns

in our day, all of us make the Lenten season a positive spiritual venture during which our prayers are made more earnest and our worship more disciplined, the whole parish and community will experience the visitation of a common spirit of kindness, caring and mutual respect. This is the real aim and focus for our keeping Lent.

Reclaiming Our Covenant

Lent 1 *Genesis 9:8-17*

How often in the secular, rough-and-tumble affairs of daily life we hear the quick suggestion, "Let's make a deal!" What does all this mean? Simply this: two persons or parties agree mutually to put a proposal equally on the line and pledge themselves to abide by the result, come what may. But something is inevitably at stake here: an assumed honesty on the part of each person involved. "I've given my word," each says. Very well, but what guarantees it? Who knows whether one party may hoodwink the other? There is always the possibility of one party having to shout, "But didn't we make a deal?"

This leads us to the realization that every deal needs a third party: an impartial individual who sees to it that the deal is fair and that it is honored by both persons who have agreed to endorse it. What is needed is that deeper element that made the ancient biblical idea of a covenant so useful and, indeed, necessary in many cases of human relationships. Covenant? What's the difference between it and a deal?

Palms and Thorns

Let us turn to the Bible and see how the idea of a covenant runs like "a golden thread" through the whole of Scripture.

In the Old Testament a covenant was more than a deal between two persons on equal terms; it was a thing of religion. God was in it. This meant that the two persons involved recognized a third party, a frame of reference, which tested the genuineness of the deal with such questions as these: Is this thing right? Is it consistent with the will of God? Indeed, the only guarantee that the deal would last was based upon the quality of the commitment of both parties to the claim upon them of the righteous will of God.

Take a look at the situation in our Scripture text: The devastating Flood was over and Noah, his family and the whole shipload of zoo creatures were let out. It had been a hectic season, confined within the Ark, tossed about on the rough waters without chart or compass or any sense of direction. But, what now? What guarantee had they that God would not pull the same thing again? "Once is enough!" would be the common outcry of the captain and crew. But their God was a covenantal God. In essence he said to Noah, "It shall never, never happen again. It's a deal. You can trust me!" The human race was to enter another new chapter and its future was underwritten by the promise of God. Noah and his people were to find in God one who bound himself in a covenant never to be broken. (v. 16) Moreover, a rainbow — always a sign that a storm was over and of unity between heaven and earth — a rainbow in the cloud would be the symbol of the integrity of the faithfulness of God.

What basic lessons, then, are here for us in the Lenten season?

1. *The idea of a covenant brings a new dimension to our human relationships.* The loss of the covenant factor can reduce many of our critical personal relationships to the level of a mere deal. Too many people enter upon an arrangement with others with the question: "What's in it for me?" With

Lent and Easter

this attitude, any concern for fairness, integrity, or lasting commitment goes out the window; or in the case of a storm or unforeseen crisis, the whole deal falls apart.

Let us bring the matter closer to home. What is at the heart of the Sacrament of Baptism for your little child? The very essence of it is that the parents take vows in God's name to expose this tiny child to the influence of the Christian faith throughout his or her youthful days. If so, God will provide the "means of grace" — the church, the Sunday school, the recognition of his presence in the home and the Christian example in the lifestyle of the parents. These channels make God's influence available, and if the parents keep their vows, God has promised to uphold his side of the covenant and will never let them or the child down.

Then, there is the wedding ceremony. The marriage vows that are exchanged between bride and groom are in essence a covenant, the most crucial part of the whole act, despite whatever tinsel and frippery our social culture has added. Such vows in the Christian context are not of the nature of "Let's make a deal." Rather they are the heart of a covenant made and said in God's name and this brings, therefore, a serious dimension to the most blessed of human relationships in which God, the bride and the groom are inextricably involved and which nothing else can supply or ever destroy.

2. *The idea of a covenant declares that the pivotal decisions in life can never be fully on our own terms.* In a deal, yes; it is no exception or surprise to hear someone ask, "What's in it for me?" Moreover, both parties can easily and readily swear to the terms of a deal, but neither may have the capacity to keep them. Human and material considerations or sheer selfish interests can break any arrangement even when one has said, "My word is my bond." But in a covenant relationship God, the third party, invites the allegiance of both persons, and in response to their commitment he supplies the ability to adhere to it. This is the peculiarly biblical

Palms and Thorns

three-way relationship in which God always holds the trump card. From our human side, then, he looks for our humble acceptance of his will for us in this event or situation and with it our gratitude for whom he is and what he does. James Reid once remarked: "We shall only know the grip of God's hand when we respond to the pull of it."[1]

Near the city of Avignon in southern France there still stands a broken-down bridge across the Rhone River. Centuries ago, on either side of the river, stood two communities which were separated by old animosities and deep-seated prejudice. It was decided to build a bridge across the river and at its mid-section a chapel was erected to remind persons as they crossed back and forth that they must take God into their hearts in order to create a friendship and make it secure.

In the old Presbyterian ritual for the Sacrament of Baptism for Infants, as he sprinkled the water, the minister said, "John Smith, child of the covenant . . . ." This meant that the child was heir to a series of covenants: God's original with his ancient people of Bible times, the covenant of the parents when they made their marriage vows and now this new step when they declared their accountability to God to bring up their child so that one day he or she will respond, "Jesus is Lord!"

Reclaim our covenant! How suitable a time is Lent for us to see to it!

---

[1]*Living in Depth* (Edinburgh: St. Andrew Press, 1959), p. 23.

Rediscovering Our
Spiritual Dimension

Lent 2 *Genesis 17:1-10, 15-19*

Nearly one hundred years ago, when Albert Einstein was merely a child and his ideas about time and space were wholly unexplored, a distinguished English headmaster, Edwin A. Abbott, wrote a strange little book titled *Flatlands*. It portrayed a peculiar world of two dimensions: a world that had length and breadth, but no height; a world of surfaces in which neither from desire nor necessity did its citizens ever look up.

Now, to us, the whole idea seems very odd, but on second thought the point becomes poignantly clear, especially when we ask ourselves this question: how many people today actually live in a two-dimensional world? Theirs is a world merely of surfaces, and they very much remind us of a remark made once by Lynn Harold Hough of Drew University about a great European house of entertainment: "The lights of the music hall have blotted out the stars."

At no time in our history has this flatness of life been more widespread and crippling than it is today. This is due largely to the fact that so frequently the aims and ends for which we live have length and breadth, but no height. Moreover, since the means we adopt to reach these ends are generally faulty, we can be blind to the further fact that the nature of the means influences almost invariably the character of the ends, and hence there has been poured into our common life an unwholesome quality that has tended to mar and discolor much of what we plan or create or produce.

Years ago, when I was a young lad, I was given a picture book depicting striking scenes from Old and New Testament literature. I remember how one of these fascinated me: a picture of Abraham gazing up wistfully one night at the millions of stars in the sky and below it the words of Genesis 15:5: "[The word of the Lord came to Abraham]: Look toward heaven, and number the stars, if you are able to number them. So shall your descendants be." (RSV) Now this scene has something of a romantic cast to it and we are apt to overlook an occasion when Abraham lapsed into the frame of mind we associate with Flatlands. Hebrew tradition emphasized the extreme and critical importance of having a son to perpetuate the family lineage in the ages to come. But Abraham did not have a son, except a foster child Ishmael, and he hoped to get by with that. God, however, had a higher plan, his own purpose for Abraham and Sarah his wife; he called Abraham to be faithful to his ancient covenant with the Hebrew people and for this a true son, Isaac, would be born to them. This was a new and startling dimension to Abraham's destiny, and it is easy for us to imagine his crying out in effect to God: "Leave me alone! I'm content with things as they are. What satisfies me, why doesn't it satisfy God?"

Now some people today think that anything in the Old Testament is far removed from and scarcely relevant to this twentieth century. But none of us needs to look very far to see that we, too, belong to a generation that chooses often to live comfortably in the region of Flatlands. Indeed, this

Lent and Easter

is a reproach against the way we exercise even our western democracy. True it is that we are free to think, speak and worship as we please, but all of this can be jeopardized if and when democracy turns its powers and advantages to serve only material goals and ends. The overall character of any democracy cannot rise any higher than the quality of life in its individual citizens and is always in special danger when its people cleave to the state of things as they are. Indeed, the biggest peril to the western world today is not who can win in shoring up selfish national interests. It lies in the inclination of the average man or woman who is content to live in a two-dimensional world. President Goheen, formerly of Princeton University, once said that much of the unrest among America's youth has tended to "show a hunger for some spiritual dimension which is all too scarce in contemporary adult American life."

In his book, *The Research Magnificent,* H. G. Wells told of a young man who regarded his life as one long succession of days that became more and more filled with aimlessness, purposelessness and shabby trivialities. Eventually for him daily life became flat, insipid and meaningless, and in his desperate plight he cried out, "O God, give me back my visions!" Do we want, while there is time, to opt out from Flatlands? Maybe it is right now in this Lenten season that we ought to begin. And for this there are three steps by which we can rediscover that needed spiritual dimension that can create in and for us a balanced life in an unbalanced world.

1. *We need a new dimension to our outlook on life.* Dietrich Bonhoeffer said, "The trouble with man is that he wants to have either God without the world or the world without God." And this disposition has divided our generation into two groups or types: the other worldly and the "me" society. But the persistence of this situation overlooks the fact that we are intended to be whole persons, that our lives must have length, breadth and spiritual height. Modern folks are

confronted by extraordinary problems: cures for social ills, solutions to nagging issues of war and peace, justice and mercy for the homeless and underprivileged, to name only a few. One group puts its hope in quickie public programs that can so easily dehumanize, while the other group scurries into a dream world of stagnant piety. Decades ago Woodrow Wilson said, "Our civilization cannot survive materially unless it be redeemed spiritually."

The New Testament, however, calls our generation to a new kind of life. True, it must have length and breadth and walk the common streets of our daily existence where it is not afraid to get its hands soiled or calloused, yet it must know that the quality and direction of its service to humanity are determined and shaped by its coming to terms with the realm of the spirit. Life for us can never be a matter of how far we can go and of how fast we can travel or of how widely and grandly we can spread ourselves — these are the works of the "me" generation with its narrow focus upon length and breadth — but if only we can catch or be caught by a vision of the spiritual dimension, we shall transcend our ordinary selves to become our real selves, to the everlasting benefit of our broken world.

2. To rediscover this spiritual dimension, *we need a new level to our faith*. Every woman or man has faith and practices faith of some kind or another. But for those people who lived in Flatlands, faith was unfortunately a cheap and mediocre thing, something mechanical that could be switched on or off whenever they got into a jam. This is the exercise of faith on only the level of length and breadth. This is, moreover, a safe business because it makes no greater demand upon us than to believe that somehow things will turn out all right. What we are and how things are is eminently safisfactory; what we *ought* to be and to do should never really be allowed to come up. Ishmael, the foster child, will do. Let Sarah live with the situation. Why allow God's purpose to

Lent and Easter

stir up the waters? It is okay to become — as John Henry Jowett put it — "like common traders in a common market babbling over common wares."

In the New Testament, however, real faith has another dimension and, therefore, it is a vigorous, exciting and risky matter. It involves grasping a vision and acting it out in spite of every consequence. It believes in and stakes its whole being upon the integrity of Christianity and its principles because it has seen the recreated person and the difference that person has made in the human situation because of his or her alliance with a divine purpose. And such is basic to Lent and to you and me to have a level of faith to believe it to be possible.

3. To rediscover life's spiritual dimension *we need the constraint of greater expectations.* Why is life so dull, humdrum and flat for so many of us these days? For so many institutions and organizations — even churches? Chiefly because our outlook upon life is marked by the absence of great expectations. True it is to say that a life-vision is necessary, and the faith to undergird it, but what gives all of it zest or a sense of excited waiting or an end to be hoped for? This was the challenge God gave Abraham as he looked up at the stars and was constrained to opt for God's purpose rather than his own.

Remember how Paul in one of his sweeping and dramatic surveys of life declared: "I have fought the good fight; I have finished the race." (2 Timothy 4:7 RSV) This indicated his prowess in the length and breadth of life. But there was more: he added, "I have kept the faith. Henceforth there is laid up for me the crown of righteousness." This was his expectation, and it gave his life a spiritual dimension that created a contagion still felt all over the earth. Because there was in him and his message this undying sense of expectation, things happened wherever he went or witnessed or spoke. Men and women throughout Asia Minor arose out of the

Palms and Thorns

ordinariness of flatlands and, sharing Paul's mission, faith and expectation, they became fit to be among the community of God's new creation.

In the Book of Revelation (chapter 21), St. John, one of the earliest of the Christian saints, had a vision of the Holy City, and he wrote: "And the city lieth foursquare: the length and the breadth and the height of it were equal." What kind of nonsense is this? What city can be as high as it is long or wide? John was thinking of its spiritual dimension and of our human expectations that nourish it. Will the generations that follow us take their quality from the extent to which you and I keep vital our covenant with God?

Restoring Our Sense of Priorities

Lent 3   Exodus 20:1-17

Whatever happened to the Ten Commandments? It is true, of course, that any one of them is trotted out on occasion to bolster an argument or to nail an offender with the rebuke, "Shame on you! Remember the Fourth (or Fifth or Sixth?) Commandment!" But what of the Ten Commandments as a whole? (The Decalogue, as biblical scholars and liturgists refer to it?) Rudyard Kipling, England's poet laureate of a hundred years ago, sang in his rollicking poem, *Mandalay:*

> *Ship me somewhere east of Suez,*
> *Where the best is like the worst,*
> *Where there aren't no Ten Commandments*
> *An' a man can raise a thirst.*

But two centuries earlier in a more serious mood, the Parish Register of a little church in Lancaster, Nottinghamshire, cited these lines:

> *Have no other gods before me;*
> *Unto no image bow the knee;*

Palms and Thorns

> *Take not the name of God in vain;*
> *Do not the Sabbath day profane;*
> *Honor thy father and mother, too;*
> *And see that thou no murder do;*
> *From vile adultery keep thou clean;*
> *And steal not, though thy state be mean;*
> *Bear no false witness — shun that blot;*
> *What is thy neighbor's covet not.*

Between these two extremes, where are we today?

In our American world of modern government, business dealings, and social matters, do the Ten Commandments figure any more? Few church members can even recite them at the drop of a hat. Most teenagers would scarcely know what we are talking about. Many older folk had memorized them from the catechism in preparation for Confirmation, but the methods of Christian educators today avoid any learning by rote, and our children are poorer for it. This eclipse of the Ten Commandments is serious. What are some of the underlying reasons for it?

1. *Some people find the Ten Commandments to be uncongenial to our present-day lifestyle.* Popular emphases are currently upon the positive. The Commandments are seemingly negative because they are laden with "Thou shalt nots." Our age responds to free expression; any kind of repression is out. Our forebears lived in an age of discipline, whereas today almost everywhere authority is suspect. The positive perspective points toward creativity, but discipline carries a freight of heavy-handed negatives. Mistakenly, many people feel that Christianity means only being *against* and they say they are not quite clear about what Christianity is *for*.

2. *The Ten Commandments fall today on the deaf ears of a generation which no longer feels the claim of a moral order upon them.* I would miss my guess if I thought the attitude of a large segment of our people toward the Ten

Lent and Easter

Commandments were not simply a matter of "So what?" And maybe such a reaction is to be expected from a generation that has for the most part pushed God out of their world. Berdyaev once remarked: "Man without God is no longer man." Humankind without God is reduced to "animalkind." Ask the Jews from the Polish ghetto or a survivor of Auschwitz! And more and nearer to home: modern literature reflects the thinking of a generation who faces the possibility of a universe without God or at best a system infused with a sort of pantheism in which God and the world are identical everywhere and in everything. An "itness" and a soullessness pervades the human as well as the material. From such a scheme no good can ever emerge, and hence "so what?" is ultimately popular and acceptable. The grim reality is that from us has gone almost any concept of a Being who loves us and therefore has a moral claim upon us, or any sense of purpose, but all is "a jumble of things going it blind" (to use Fosdick's phrase), with nothing that cares, and hence we feel no pull of any ultimate meaning to life. There is no rationale whatsoever for the Ten Commandments in an outlook such as that.

3. *Our idea of Christian love has been reduced to a level of sentimentality.* Love has been taken over by either of two modern concepts, both of which are wrong. Love, according to the "pop" singers, is a matter of emotion only; it has no depth, no fiber, no lasting quality any more than froth. Then there are the televangelists whose idea of love is something without any cost. It's merely a good fellow feeling. But to rise to the high level of Christian love it must involve caring, justice and outreach — sometimes at a fearful price. Otherwise it is sheer sentimentality without any ethical framework. This is where the Ten Commandments come in. They supply the road map for living, and the Gospel of the New Testament gives us the will and the spirit to abide by them. Remember Paul's dilemma: "For I do not the good I

Palms and Thorns

want, but the evil I do not want is what I do . . . Who shall deliver me? . . . Thanks be to God through Jesus Christ." (Romans 7:19, 24 RSV) Our "me" generation says trippingly off its tongue, "God loves you and so do I." But, frankly, it should be more than this; it should read, "Since God loves us we should love him and our neighbor as ourselves." And such love demands heart, soul, strength and mind — dimensions we avoid or neglect too easily.

On what basis then do we make a case for the Ten Commandments? Simply this: "In the Ten Commandments we have two principal basics to our religious lifestyle: our accountability 1. to God, and 2. to our neighbor.

1. *The Ten Commandments are essential to cancelling out our mishandling of life's priorities.* Note how the Commandments begin: "Thou shalt have no other gods before me." Every one of us worships something. This is true of human nature. But it is to our peril when we give our allegiance to many gods. Hence our besetting sin becomes idolatry. Once we criticized the heathen in their blindness bowing down "to wood and stone." But idolatry is the worship of anything other than God. Our idols today are money, class, power, success, prestige and all the other things that claim our devotion totally. For every Christian God must have first place or else he has no place. Whatever we value most in life will be what we worship, and it is by and from this that our conduct and character are determined.

Moreover, this God we worship is not an unknown being. We see him in the face of Jesus Christ, for as one theologian has put it, "God always was what he was in Christ Jesus." And through Christ, God sought to bring the world back to himself, a world that had broken his laws and put themselves first in the gallery of their devotions. The Ten Commandments declare as our basic need our accountability to God for whom he is and what he has done for us.

Lent and Easter

2. *The Ten Commandments outline our second priority: our accountability to the whole world of men and women everywhere.* The first four commandments spell out our accountability to God; the next six embrace our duty to humankind. These six are not, however, mere social actions with no greater moral claim than "Be kind to grandmother and the cat." They are the outgrowth of the first four. In other words, the quality and meaning of our worship of God find their results in the kind of treatment we make and give to our fellow human beings. If our worship is perfunctory, then our service to other persons will not be praiseworthy. It is not worthwhile to know what to do unless we have the will to do it. And this is the ultimate contribution Christianity brings, namely, that in and through Christ we get the power to perform what the Commandments urge us to do and to be. In *The Book of Common Prayer* at the end of the Confirmation Service, the minister says:

> *Go forth into the world in peace; be of good courage; hold fast to what is good; render to no person evil for evil; strengthen the faint hearted; support the weak; help the afflicted; honor all people, love and serve the Lord, rejoicing in the power of the Holy Spirit.*

Reviving Our
Moral Responsibility

Lent 4 *2 Chronicles 36:14-23*

Some years ago I spent several weeks during the summer indexing and classifying the Scripture texts in all the volumes of published sermons on my study shelves. Many interesting trends and preferences emerged from this tabulation; for example, among some four thousand printed sermons only two preachers had ever done a sermon from the Book of Chronicles. And little wonder, someone might very well say. Here is an Old Testament book which in sixty-five chapters attempts an accounting of a confused and confusing mishmash of the careers of ancient Jewish kings, priests and military figures with all their intrigues, double-dealings, moral escapades and tribal warfare against a wide backdrop of God's judgments and blessings.

This leads us to the final verses of the last chapter of 2 Chronicles. (36:11-23) Here, yet another king, Zedekiah — a mere boy of twenty-one years — reigned in Jerusalem for just a short term of eleven years. But what a sad story this brief rule unfolds! Listen to it: "He did what was evil in the sight of the Lord his God;" (v. 12) "he did not humble himself before Jeremiah the prophet who spoke from the mouth of the Lord;" and "he hardened his heart against turning to the God of Israel." (v. 13) But this was not the only problem. The throne and the altar were the twin centers of Israel's life. And now the religious leaders themselves were depraved and degenerate in the acquittal of their office. They had become out-and-out idolaters, and behind the scenes in the Temple they allowed heathen practices to pollute the purity of Israel's religion. While prophets warned the kings and priests against God's judgment coming upon them, yet we read they "mocked the messengers of God" (v. 16) and "scoffed" at predictions of trouble ahead.

God, however, gave them all the rope they wanted and they took it. But they didn't realize that you cannot push God up against the wall. In all of biblical history God has used others — other nations, other events, other crises — to advance his purpose or to reveal his displeasure. To teach Israel a lesson he chose the King of Babylon to bring Israel to its knees. His armies devastated the land, destroyed the Temple, stole its sacred treasures and carried off a large segment of the population into captivity for seventy years.

Now: Does this slab of ancient history have anything to say to us in this concluding decade of the twentieth century? And more particularly, what basics for living are called here to our attention in this Lenten period?

1. *We are responsible to a moral order that we defy or disregard at our peril.* We are living in a time when order of any kind appears to be the least of all realities. Indeed it seems at times that the bottom has dropped out of everything. The ideals and hopes that Christians have held dear seem to be caught up in a whirlwind of opposing forces bent on their destruction. Christians believe in love, but everywhere throughout the world we see the fingerprints of the agents of hate. Christians affirm the power of right, but others claim that might is the only resource with any viable clout.

Lent and Easter

Christians are apostles of goodness and kindness, yet their witness is overshadowed by reports of child abuse, domestic violence, homelessness, political intrigue and deception even in high places. It would seem at times that to preach love as a redeeming power is to prattle a sheer fiction or is as useless as howling against the wind.

There is an old saying from our American poet, Longfellow: "The mills of God grind slowly." Consider, for example, the prodigal in Jesus' parable: he carried the spirit of rebellion, disloyalty and loose living to their logical conclusion and discovered neither happiness nor fulfillment, but sorry defeat in a pig sty. Why so? Simply because there is a moral order in this universe which says, "You reap what you sow." And if this order cannot be trusted, the idea of a good and righteous God is nonsense. Look at it this way: if it were not for the dependability of such a moral and spiritual order, and if people and nations could continue to live selfishly and recklessly and still end up at the Gates of Life, then who could have faith in God?

Is this not what our pericope from the Book of Chronicles is all about? It's a drama in which a people are being held responsible for the disorder of their times. Who did they think God was? St. Paul wrote, "Behold the goodness and severity of God." (Romans 11:22 RSV) Our God is both. Were he good without severity, he'd be an indulgent, fuddy-duddy being; and if he were severe without goodness, he'd be a cruel God. And our God is neither. Moreover, as long as God is such, there exists in the whole scheme of things a moral necessity to which we are held responsible. And we are irresponsible when we raise millions of dollars to cure disease, feed the hungry, house the homeless, and at the same time spend billions upon lethal weapons to destroy — whom? Well, we're not quite sure. People criticize the Middle Ages and certainly they had their faults. But it was in a sense the age of Christendom. Its center of reference was God and the people's

Palms and Thorns

response to this great reality is seen in the monuments of art and architecture and literature they left behind. But something is missing in our day. Jeremiah touched on it when he wrote: "I know that man's ways are not of his own choosing; nor is it for a man to determine his course in life." (Jeremiah 10:23 NEB) This is what we've been doing. Like the kings and priests of Israel, we have been eager to hold for our own selves the whole scheme of things, while we have neglected the moral and spiritual order by which we should be held. If you and I break the laws of nature, eventually and surely we break ourselves against them. Our world is "out of joint" today. Does this mean that God has ceased to care for it? Certainly not! The proper question is: Have we been fully responsible to those eternal laws by which God steers his world?

2. This would be a sorry state of affairs were it not for the second lesson the Book of Chronicles leaves with us. *God's judgments do come when we defy his moral and spiritual order, but they are not his final word.* He points his finger at us accusingly, but when he has made his point, the finger bends into a beckoning gesture: Follow me in obedience and I will give you a new life. It is on this note that the Book of Chronicles ends. It concludes with a forecast of the returning exiles to a new community with endless possibilities for those who will walk with God. To the extent that they are obedient, they will realize that they are God's people, a God whose word is true, and in whose land they will realize the fulfillment of their lives.

Each Lenten season calls our generation to the same course of obedience. This is the positive side of Lent. It is always positive to be responsible.

Returning to Genuine Religion

Lent 5 *Jeremiah 31:31-34*

There is a simple poem by Louise F. Tarkington which goes in part this way:

> *I wish there were some wonderful place*
> *Called the Land of Beginning Again,*
> *Where all our mistakes and all our heartaches*
> *Could be dropped like a shabby old coat at the door*
> *And never put on again.*

What has this to do with the return of the Jewish exiles from seventy years in slavery in Babylon? Everything! Because, as they left Babylon behind and turned their faces toward their homeland, they carried a lot of mental baggage along with them. They had the backward look. They had the memory of suffering through several generations — humiliation, painful separation from their religious centers, daily encounters with people who prized false gods and bowed down to idols, and the sight of a new generation of their own people emerging with the taint upon them of Babylonian culture, superstition and even lifestyle. And what was more: they were haunted by some basic questions — Why had their God permitted them to be carried off into slavery in the first place? What guarantee was given that it might not happen again? They were haunted by the old proverb: "The fathers have eaten sour grapes, and the children's teeth are set on edge." (Jeremiah 31:29) They wondered whether this maxim was still intact.

God seemed, however, at this point to do a turnaround, and happily so. It were as if a new reel were put into the machine and on the screen the future was forecast. And it was a joy to behold. God promised a healing process, and with it a new era was opening up. Note the verbs in these passages: "restore," "return," "renew," "rebuild," "forgive," and so on. Judah and Israel were to be restored to their own land, the Temple was to be rebuilt, a new age of freedom and independence was in the offing, and one of their own kin would rule them. "There is hope for the future, says the Lord." (v. 17) Blessings would be the new lot of Israel and they would become a blessing to others.

All these things, however, were not to occur or become theirs by mere fiat. True, God had declared his readiness to establish a new covenant with his people. (v. 31) But, as you and I know, a covenant requires the commitment of two parties. God's promise must be met by the honest avowal of every individual and not merely as a resolution passed by the people as at a mass meeting. This had been a fault in Israel's religious life in the past. The priests ran the system and all the people had to do was to perform small ritual duties in order to keep their membership intact. Like the religion of the Pharisees or the pre-Reformation church, for example: Attend certain feasts or check in once a year at Easter or perform certain negotiations during Lent, and all would be OK. Religion was managed for these Israelites and all they had to do was inject oil into the machine. This is always a

Lent and Easter

recipe for spiritual paralysis. As John Paterson remarked: "A religion of the book inevitably supplants the religion of the Spirit."[1] Or, "You can't make people right by an Act of Congress."

At this point God took positive action. A new covenant was to be initiated because the people were unable as a people to live up to the letter of the ancient Law. A totally new scheme of things was to become operative, different from the rigid legalism of the past; it was to be now a channel for God's grace. The returning exiles were to become God's own people, (v. 33) be shaped by his Word and live independently in his land.

What, then, did all this mean to the religion of Israel?

1. *Each person was to be responsible directly to God.* A new dimension was to emerge in Israel's religion. It would forecast an era of personal religion. Up to now, religion had been apt to be an external thing, gauged and evaluated by the rule of Law, a matter of punching the clock daily and making sure it was done on time. But now God said through his prophet, Jeremiah, "I will put my law within them and I will write it upon their hearts." (v. 33) Changed lives would no longer come by Law, for hitherto such a process led inevitably to self-righteousness. Whereas with personal religion, each man or woman must stand as a naked soul before God whose grace would reach into the very depths of their being and reckon once and for all with their sin and pride. Personal religion, moreover, would be then a first-hand matter; it was not to be simply what had been told by others, but what each soul learned and felt for himself or herself. (v. 34) Remember Jesus' question of Pilate: "Do you say this of your own accord, or did others say it to you about me?" (John 18:34 RSV) This means that each of us must be touched individually by God and be able as a result to witness from his or her own heart. Each is constrained to do right, not because some Law requires it, but as the expression of one's inner conviction and desire.

Palms and Thorns

2. This leads us to a second point: *The spirit in which Israel's religion was to be lived and exercised.* Do you ever wonder why many Americans obey the law? Because they are so morally good? Because they might harm someone else? No! They observe the law because they are afraid of being caught. It's as simple as that! Something similar was inherent in Israel's religion of the Law. Remember how Luke put it concerning the Pharisees and Jesus: "The Pharisees . . . , lying in wait for him, to catch at something he might say." (11:54 RSV) Religion ruled by the Law was rigid, creating suspicion and tempting people to snitch on one another. But with Israel's return from exile and bondage, God's new covenant spelled out religion as a liberating experience, no longer a matter of being dominated by rules. Hence a new factor was inserted: the element of joy. "Sing for joy, O heavens, and exult, O earth; break forth, O mountains into singing! . . . For behold I create new heavens and a new earth and the former things will not be remembered . . . . But be glad and rejoice forever in that which I create; for behold, I create Jerusalem a rejoicing, and her people a joy." (Isaiah 49:13; 66:17, 18 RSV) Can't you sense in these lines the elements of happiness, enjoyment and the contagion of a new brand of fellowship with God? Begone to such warnings as "The goblins will get you if you don't watch out!" Henceforth, with the words of the Psalmist, people would say, "I delight to do thy will, O my God." (Psalm 40:8 RSV)

And we who live on this side of the New Testament know how this religion in and of the heart marked the ministry and witness of Jesus. Of him and his company, Arthur J. Gossip wrote:

> *Always they stood upon the threshold of happy hours, always a door was opening upon such glorious things, and every day that dawned let in new crowding opportunities of ever gladder service.*[2]

Lent and Easter

Then, a third observation: *We must not overlook the "givenness" of it all.* Emerson once said, "I did not find my friends; the good God gave them to me." So, with the nature of genuine religion. And this Israel was to learn: the fruits of true religion are realized not through the number of your cultic sacrifices, nor by the vicious circle of performing endless rituals in some rigidly appropriate ways, nor by standing before the world with a holy face and declaring, "Thou shalt not!" A great reversal was now afoot: prior to Israel's offering of sheep and goats in ritual sacrifices, God had already given. His love and grace were already in the field, claiming these people as his own. This is why we see in Jeremiah 31 this new covenant as the closest the Old Testament comes to the gospel of the New Testament. It is the religion of the changed heart. And for the realization of all this, God would make the offering of his Son who through his ministry, his witness to eternal love and his life of reconciliation would see it finally by his Resurrection.

The old Gospel hymn puts it rightly:

Amazing grace! How sweet the sound
That saved a wretch like me!
I once was lost, but now am found,
Was blind, but now I see.

'Twas grace that taught my heart to fear,
And grace my fears relieved;
How precious did that grace appear
The hours I first believed!
 (John Newton, 1979)

Here, moreover, lies our Lenten obligation. You and I must, in response, dedicate to God our life. Lent is part of a larger and longer pilgrimage in which we go on seeking a city "whose builder and maker is God." The ancient Law

Palms and Thorns

written on tables of stone must be replaced by the law written upon our heart. Outer nature can be governed by rules, but our inner nature calls for harmony with the will of God. The elder brother in Jesus' parable could run the farm efficiently by rules, but to come into the fellowship of the father's home, his younger brother had to say, "I have sinned."

---

[1] *The Goodly Fellowship of the Prophets* (New York: Charles Scribner's Sons, 1948 pp. 149, 150.

[2] *From the Edge of the Crowd* (Edinburgh: T & T. Clark, 1926), p. 153.

Reconciling
Palms and Thorns

The Sunday of the Passion/   *Isaiah 50:4-9a*
Palm Sunday

Great days are a typical event in the life story of any people. Every nation has a calendar date when they stop, look and listen, accompanied by a backward glance momentarily upon the way by which they have come. We Americans have our Fourth of July; the French, their Bastille Day; and the English — they have so many Victoria, Waterloo, Trafalgar, and so on. Earlier than any of those were the ancient Jews, and among their revered traditions was especially the day of liberation from Egyptian bondage. Great days for the Jews, however, had a dimension often overlooked in ours: their great days kept both past and future in focus. The past reminded them of a time of deliverance, while the future held up a vista of the realization of national and religious ideals. Past deliverances were signs of God's blessing, acts of God's grace and favor, while the future called for fulfillment of the people's obligations and responsibilities. It was easy for them to say, "God has done great things for us whereof we are glad," (Psalm 126:3 RSV) but the hard factor lay in realizing and fulfilling the measure of accountability involved.

Palms and Thorns

Let us not miss seeing how this idea has relevance to us and our way of life today. We Americans have spent two centuries attempting to fulfill a national dream, but unfortunately our product or output is largely material. It is easy to glory in all this, but it is equally easy to lose sight of what is involved here, "What are we here for?" "What is our mission, if anything?" We have heard our leaders say, "Life, liberty, and the pursuit of happiness"; "I have a dream"; "We demand our 'rights.' " President Reagan in his farewell message to the nation (January 11, 1989) remarked: "If we forget what we did, we won't know who we are . . . [and] that could result in an erosion of the American spirit." It is easy on occasion to rise to an emotional peak, but what about the next day, the next year, the future destiny? This raises the question of our mission as a people and as individuals and equally important: the price we are willing to pay to realize it.

Our scripture lessons today indicate interesting parallels between situations centuries apart. There was the Old Testament prophet, Isaiah, who was stirred by an unusual conception of mission — whether of his people or himself or some future messianic figure, we do not know — in which he singled out the attitudes and characteristics that would play a large and basic part in it. Listen to these phrases: "That I may know how to sustain with a word him that is weary"; (v. 4) "I was not rebellious, I turned not backward. I gave my back to the smiters"; (v. 5) "I have set my face like a flint"; (v. 7) "I know that I shall not be put to shame; he who vindicates me is near." (v. 8) This sense of mission quickened his determination even though he was realistic enough to recognize that it involved a price.

We skip now over seven centuries and come to the mission of Jesus, and we read phrases reminiscent of the career of the ancient prophet. Listen to the writers of the New Testament: "He set his face steadfastly to go to Jerusalem"; "I must work the works of him who sent me while it is day";

Lent and Easter

"If any would come after me, let them deny themselves and take up their cross and follow me"; . . . I lay down my life for the sheep. And I have other sheep . . . I must bring them also . . . So there shall be one flock, one shepherd."

Today is the final Sunday in the Lenten Season of the Church Year. It is known either as Palm Sunday or Passion Sunday. But it is really both, for it blends two portraits of Jesus: the Jesus of Palms and the Jesus of Thorns. There is the Jesus we accept readily and there is the Jesus we need but find difficult and costly to follow. Let us be honest with ourselves: Are we not inclined to be like the crowds on that first Palm Sunday? Excited over his miracles of healing, his concern for the poor and underprivileged, his love for those whom sin had almost destroyed, and his personal popularity with the multitudes, these people in a quick flush of emotion were ready to call Jesus their King. Picture, if you will, his entering that day into Jerusalem, the nation's capital, seated upon a donkey, surrounded by throngs of the faithful who waved palm branches and shouted: "Hosanna! Blessed be he who comes in the name of the Lord . . . Hosanna in the highest!" This is the kind of popular Jesus the crowd wanted, but how taken aback they must have been when so soon afterwards he looked down upon the city and wept over it, saying: "Would that even today you knew the things that make for peace!" And then he came to the Temple and in an angry sweep he upset the tables of the money changers, the bingo players and the black marketeers, crying: "My house shall be called a house of prayer, but you have made it into a den of robbers!"

We, too, are fond of the Jesus of Palms. We talk and sing about "Gentle Jesus, meek and mild," of the shy little Jesus boy, and of the woolly Lamb of God. And our artists and painters have sketched the face of Jesus as soft and smooth, replacing the rugged and robust features with anemic and pallid colors. We fill our economy gift shops with cheap and

Palms and Thorns

tawdry religious souvenirs that belong to the mediocre levels of our culture. Our Jesus is made into a pseudo-magician who steps into the human situation whenever we get into a jam. It costs little to accept a Jesus like that.

The sorry condition of our modern world demands that we say, "Enough of this!" The time is emergent for us to see that the Jesus of Palms is never fully adequate for the eternal mission to the world until he becomes for us the Jesus of Thorns, that is, until we are ready and willing to go along with him at the risk and price of a cross. Therefore, as we enter this Holy Week of 1991, we must accept the claims of his mission among us, and for us and for this he must become the actuating principle in all of our life.

What we see, then, is plainly this: we can never understand who Jesus is or what his mission to the world means until we reconcile the Jesus of Palms with the Jesus of Thorns. Only by our accepting such a Jesus will we be able to witness to the whom and what and why of his wondrous life. This is all the more needful because our world is full of people who are all too ready to tell Jesus what his job is. That is, for example, the "peace of mind" group who think of Christianity as being merely a prescription to assure us of tranquility or to provide a sort of emotional neutrality in which our harried souls can relax. Would not Jesus make short shrift of this point by saying, "I came not to bring peace but a sword."? Or, there is the "idealism" group who say, "Well, after all, Jesus gave us a great ideal to live up to." Once John H. Withers of Belfast, Ireland, was discussing this type and remarked, "Never was there a century in which idealism was as high as today, yet humanity staggers in drunken incompetence from one calamity to the next." Or, there is the "problem" group, who declare that Jesus was the great problem-solver, as if he were some sort of celestial mechanic who could be called down whenever our motor begins to sputter. The real Jesus — the Jesus of Palms and

Lent and Easter

Thorns — was none of these! And if any of these had been the aim of his mission, it would not have been worthwhile for him to come at all.

If this Lenten season means anything at all to us, it has to mean a closer walk with God. But we shall miss out on its saving and transforming significance if it becomes for us nothing more than a nostalgic waving of palms and shouting of Alleluias on the Jerusalem road. Emil Brunner has said, "We cannot live *without* God. But also we cannot live *with* God as long as our sins have not been removed."

Cecil Alexander, the hymn-writer joins us here, singing:

He died that we might be forgiven,
He died to make us good,
That we might go at last to heaven,
Saved by his precious blood.

And Jesus himself knew, as he set his face like a flint to go to Jerusalem, that before the crucial encounter between evil and the redeeming and reconciling love of God would be resolved, it would take inevitably the shape of the Cross. For his mission was to turn all humankind from sin to good, from wrong to right, from death to life, and the only way to do it was to invest himself completely in the lives he claimed as his own. And when love goes that far, it defies verbal description and can only be symbolized by the Cross.

James S. Stewart of Edinburgh tells how the name of Bishop Hannington has always been linked with the first Christian mission in Uganda, East Africa. He was killed by the natives, but just when the emissaries of the African chieftain came to do him to death, he shouted, "Go and tell your king that I will open up the road to Uganda *with my life!*"

This is the kind of life intimated by a faithful observance of Lent. This is the way the divine love acts. It identifies itself with us in Christ so that by faith we can go on identifying

Palms and Thorns

ourselves in his mission with him. And this is no mission for the little men and women of the world. It is only for the strong who embrace the Jesus of Palms and then go on to commit themselves to the claims and example of the Jesus of Thorns.

Cecil Alexander sang further:

O dearly, dearly has he loved,
And we must love him too,
And trust in his redeeming love
And try his works to do.
(1823-1895)

And Thomas Kelly's couplet is appropriate:

The Head that once was crowned with thorns
Is crowned with glory now.
(1769-1854)

Servants Without Fiber

Monday *Isaiah 42:1-9*

A biblical scholar once remarked: "One of the most common expressions in the Old Testament of the relationship between humankind and God is contained in the words 'serve,' 'service,' and 'servant.'" What comes to your mind when you hear any one of these words? What do you think of when you hear the word "servant"? A flunky? A gofer? A Victorian called "Jeeves"? Someone with no mind of his or her own? A person who lacks fiber and is easily a patsy for someone else to use or "lord it over"? Unfortunately, in too many cases, people are inclined to think in this way.

But this has never been the biblical concept which emerges gradually in the Old Testament and is perfected in the New. The Bible rescued and redefined the concept of "servant," giving it fiber, stamina and spiritual substance. Probably no writer discussed the servant idea more fully than the prophet Isaiah, and what he wrote cast a long ray of understanding across the people and events of biblical witness and history. The servant could be a nation, a ruler or a religious leader, but in God's good time it came to its

Palms and Thorns

ultimate expression in the person of Jesus Christ and his mission to the whole wide world. For us today, however, what matters is the character of servanthood and how it shapes a sense of who we are and what our lives are about, really. Of the many things Isaiah says of the servant whose inner character has real fiber, there are three which are appropriate emphases during this Holy Week.

1. *The servant is not a loner;* he does not move and live in solitary. Nor is he a freewheeler. Neither is he a miscellaneous activist, rushing around putting out brush fires or giving handouts here and there in order to foster good feeling or to be blinking as one of a thousand points of light with no unity of effort or established ends. Isaiah, instead, sees the true servant as one who has an orientation to God's ordering and control. Hear his opening words in our text: "My servant whom I uphold, my chosen, in whom my soul delights . . . ." (Isaiah 42:1 RSV) Clearly the servant is not ever his or her own. There is a givenness about the servant's character; the servant is endowed with qualifications that come from an order and will beyond self and which lay claim upon every personal talent and power. As Prof. G. Ernest Wright expressed it: "[It is] God's reaching down into human affairs."[1] Or, as it is stated more fully in *The Speaker's Bible:*

> *The servant of the Lord is useful only because he is used; influential only because he is influenced; victorious because he is obedient; learning the methods of his work by daily wakefulness to God's voice; a good speaker because he is a good listener, with no strength or courage but what God lends.*[2]

2. Here is a second emphasis: *the servant has a sense of direction in his or her calling.* The servant comes upon the human scene as one whose purpose is to set things right. And the remarkable thing is the attitude of the true servant as

he or she goes about the assigned task. Listen to these lines: "He will not cry or lift up his voice . . . a bruised reed he will not break, and a dimly burning wick he will not quench; he will faithfully bring forth justice. He will not fail or be discouraged till he has established justice in the earth." (vv 2-4) What a wonderful combination there is here of means and ends! The servant has a high purpose, but knows that the character of the means will determine the character of the ends. The servant's intention is to heal and repair whatever and whoever is hurting or broken, but it will not be done through a rough-and-ready style. Every act of helplessness must be done with a larger and higher purpose in mind.

This leads us to re-think much of the social action and public welfare programs of our day. In the face of the crying needs of our time — poverty, homelessness, joblessness and so forth — it is not enough to simply give a cup of cold water — which for many a giver is a matter simply of self-satisfaction or an escape from the program. Social service must not become a substitute for religion. Christianity is not merely helping people. Such quick fixes produce persons who are generous in contributing to the Community Fund, but who scorn the church and avoid its worship. They fail to see that service without religion becomes materialistic and that religion without service becomes something unreal. True, the servant gives the needy a cup of cold water, but note what Jesus added to this remark: "in the name of a disciple"; (Matthew 10:42 RSV) that is, the act of helpfulness is done in the name of something of universal moral and spiritual significance. The giver gives because he or she is reaching out to a sister or brother in a world where God is Creator, Father and Redeemer. The deepest need of the needy lies within. And, therefore, a mere cup of cold water does not lift his or her spirit out of the pit into which poverty, injustice, drugs or other misery has thrown them. The question, then, is: Does our service speak some message? That of the true servant does, because its central purpose is to invest the redeeming power of our religious conviction into the life of the person in need, so that it will bring him or her to the fullness of the self-realization of personal abilities, talents and potential. A cup of cold water only prolongs an unfortunate situation. What a difference there is when the aim and purpose of the servant is to advance a Kingdom in which everyone can find their place!

3. A third, and final thought: *the true servant brings a measure of dignity to every act of service.* For this we turn to the New Testament and look at our Lord as he combined a venture in humility with an act of genuine service. To wash another's feet was the duty of a slave, but Jesus was never so conscious of his high calling as when he — to quote John's Gospel — "knowing . . . that he had come from God and was going to God, rose from supper, laid aside his garments, and girded himself with a towel . . . and began to wash the disciples' feet . . . ." (John 13:4, 5 RSV) This demonstrates for us forever that the quality of service depends upon the spirit in which it is done. Our service will have fiber and contagion if it is inspired by a calling and purpose which God alone can provide and bless.

---

[1]*Isaiah,* Layman's Bible Commentary, Vol. 11, p. 105 (Richmond: John Knox, 1964)

[2]*The Book of Isaiah,* Vol. 2, p. 45 (Grand Rapids, MI; Baker Book House, 1963)

Service Beset by "What's the Use?"

Tuesday   *Isaiah 49:1-6*

In one of his poems, John Greenleaf Whittier wrote these lines:

> *Of all sad words of tongue or pen,*
> *The saddest are these: It might have been.*

Today, if we were asked to rewrite Whittier's lines to reflect the mood of many people, we might put it this way:

> *Of all sad words that are on the loose,*
> *The saddest are these: What's the use?*

Some years ago in Chicago, a parish minister sent out hundreds of questionnaires to people in every walk of life. He received a surprisingly great response, all of which he carefully indexed and tabulated. In each questionnaire only one point was raised: What is the outstanding problem or question you face daily in your thinking or living? Twenty-two percent named their family. Forty-eight percent mentioned personal living: the seemingly loneliness, general failure and futility of it all.

On the bulletin board of an Ivy League university, this item appeared: "WANTED — a young couple to care for an elderly millionaire who has been taking tranquilizers for twenty years. The need is desperate in order to give him meaning to life. He has nothing to live for."

All of these instances have a common factor that can be expressed in one word: futility. This mood is reflected again and again in our human story, and the Bible is no exception. In the fourth verse of the forty-ninth chapter of Isaiah, we hear a cry of discouragement from this great prophet: "I have labored in vain. I have spent my strength for nothing . . . ." Now, for more than a half-century the people of Israel had been exiles in pagan Babylon. But God had not abandoned them, for a new chapter of their history was beginning to emerge: out of the north came Cyrus, the Persian warrior, whose pressures on the Babylonian Empire eroded its strongholds and set the captives free. What a tremendous hour for the prophet! Now his hopes were being fulfilled and his prophecies vindicated. God had intervened and opened up a highway for the exiles to return to Jerusalem and rebuild their Temple as a free nation. Well might he sing: "Lift up your voice with strength . . . fear not. Say to the cities of Judah, 'Behold your God!' " (Isaiah 40:9)

But people everywhere are human, and even the best of us can be disappointing. Some of these exiles refused to return home; they were at ease amid a climate of idolatry. Others were in favor of moving out, but were so slow and disorganized that they tried the prophet's optimism and patience. And some others tried compromise; they got into stride, but were thoughtlessly bringing their pagan gods with them. Is it not surprising, then, that Isaiah, witnessing the slow reaction of his people, should be hurled momentarily into the pit of depression and dejection and should reveal

Lent and Easter

his inner feeling in these words: "I have labored in vain. I have spent my strength for nothing . . . ." Life seemed pointless and useless. Where was the result for his labor? Was there no rhyme nor reason to all his toil?

This was an intimation of futility away back, twenty-six centuries ago. Yet futility still holds many people in amazing numbers in its grip today. Despite all the benefits of science, culture and progress, more often than not we are a confused, bewildered and frustrated generation. Martin Buber, the great Jewish philosopher, was describing once the temperament of the people of Europe and he said, "They are working hard, but they are working in the dark." Whatever excuse may be given for such a state of mind in Europe, it stirs our curiosity when this disease of futility appears to be rampant today among vast numbers of Americans who have everything they want. Every day on our streets we meet people who seem to be going through the motions of living as if an ominous catastrophe were just around the corner. How one misses the uplifted face, the flashing eye and the shoulders braced and squared with courage. Many seem to believe like old Sorrell in Warwick Deeping's novel, "Man is fighting a lone fight against a vast indifference." Or, as one Englishman cried, "What is the point of trying to be Christian when the devil holds all the trump cards?" Something has seemingly gone out of our lives, and into the vacuum has come the deadening mood of futility. And this problem is not political, economic or national — it is basically moral and spiritual. For if people could believe greatly in something, if they could see the outline of a purpose that would give reason to daily living, then life would wear the radiant image of victory.

By now you ask: what has Isaiah to do with all this? If he was the victim of futility amid the simplicities of his life, what does he have to say to the complex situation we face

Palms and Thorns

in this twentieth century? Simply this: although he was assailed by adversity in its bitterest form, yet he met it head on and defeated it because he was equipped with certain fundamentals — not just ten little rules for confident living — but inner convictions that came from observing the way God acts with men and women who are obedient to his will. Let us look, then, at three of these that are suggested in this passage of scripture and see for ourselves what sustained the prophet in his struggle with futility.

1. Isaiah had the conviction that *he had a place of significance and worth in human society.* Note in the first verse how he puts it: "From my birth God had made mention of my name." Is not this a missing note in much of our thinking today? Constantly we are told to safeguard the worth of other individuals — and rightly so — but the climate and conditions of our age should persuade us to see also the worth of ourselves. Too many people are inclined to treat themselves as non-entities, as mere statistics in the human struggle, and forget to believe and see that they are members of God's great family and that the quality of the whole depends upon the quality of each single unit in it. If you believe that this universe is merely an accident or that life is (as one student put it), "a bad joke that isn't even funny," then it is folly to be concerned about one's self or anyone else. But if you believe that it was God who called you into being, you will see life from a new perspective, yourself endowed with a new purpose and captured by a new meaning, and then you will want to make your life morally and spiritually great in order to count 100% in God's plan. "From your birth God has made mention of your name." When you and I believe this, there is no room for futility and no one of us will feel that our work and witness are in vain.

2. Isaiah had another conviction: *he was an instrument in the hands of God.* Note in verse 3 how he reports God's word to his own life: "Thou art my servant in whom I will

Lent and Easter

be glorified." While Isaiah was concerned about the task of counselling and encouraging his own people, he believed that the truth of God was being expressed through his words and caring. The Westminster Shorter Catechism says: "God is Spirit, infinite, eternal and unchangeable in his being, wisdom, power, holiness, justice, goodness and truth." And just as light requires a surface to reflect it, else it is not seen, so also God's way and will are reflected in human witness and character. Therefore, when we do what is wise rather than indiscreet; when we commit our lives to justice rather than unfairness; and when we seek truth rather than falsehood, we are on the side of God, doing his will and through us he breaks into glory. The late John A. Mackay once remarked: "We become related to Christ singly, but we cannot live in Christ solitarily." Commitment to God in Christ directs our lives ever outward to work his purpose for all people. And when we are so engaged, the thrill of our enthusiasm outstrips any assault by futility.

3. Isaiah had another conviction: *he felt he could trust God's handling of tomorrow.* Note his words in verse 4: "Yet surely my judgment is with the Lord and my work with my God." He gave it all over to God and thus conquered any sense of futility. He took Kierkegaard's "leap of faith." Oh, but people interrupt and protest, "This is what all you preachers say — simply have faith and all will be well!" But these people who say this are usually not sure of what faith is; for them it means believing in what you know to be untrue. If that be so, then no scientist, inventor or explorer would have ever budged an inch and we would still be living in caves. But the men and women of real faith have been those whose motto has been, in Frederick Buechner's words, "Hold fast by letting go." Or, as William Barclay put it: "It is the man who is in a right relationship with God as a result of his faith who really lives." At one time in Africa David Livingstone felt his work was hopeless, futile and in vain,

Palms and Thorns

but it was then that he fell back on Christ's promise, "Lo, I am with you, even unto the end of the world." And later he wrote in his diary, "These are the words of a man of the most sacred and strictest honor." There is a point in living! How happy we can be if and when we find it.

Service Without Witness

Wednesday   *Isaiah 50:4-9a*

Most worshiping Christians are familiar with at least that part of a wonderful prayer by St. Francis of Assisi that goes this way:

> *Lord, make me an instrument of Thy peace. Where there is hatred, let me sow love. Where there is injury, pardon. Where there is doubt, faith. Where there is despair, hope. Where there is darkness, light. Where there is sadness, joy.*[1]

These words reach into the deepest meaning of service, but note this very significant feature: St. Francis combines serving with being. Many people, even among church members, think that running to and fro in a fever of busyness is the sum total of true service. Nothing is further from the truth. It can avoid such important questions as these: Does who and what we are color the helpfulness of our doing? What is the end note of our serving?

Palms and Thorns

Remember Jesus' remark: "Those who are well have no need of a physician, but those who are sick." (Matthew 9:12 RSV) In our serving, do we give greater attention to those who are well and whole rather than to those in genuine need? It was said of Plato that his message was for the "noble and good." His theory of the ideal State was good, but in his opinion it could be created only by cultured, refined, well-bred people. He had little use for the poor, the ignorant and the sinful. Indeed Judaism, too, leaned in a similar direction. It worked well with the morally righteous but not with the broken, outcast, publicans and sinners.

It is interesting to note that Isaiah, in discussing the mission of the servant, said it was directed to the "weary." (v. 4) And isn't this same emphasis germane today? Tuesday we talked about those for whom life seems futile. Our scripture text today is concerned with another type of person: those for whom life is a drag, a program of dull monotony, a slow trek that is hurting and sore. These must be the focus of our service today. They are troubled. For many of them the load is heavy and gradually they have lost heart. They wonder if they are forever doomed. To be servant to them is not easy, and we would prefer to minister to people who are vigorous and strong. One day a Scottish layman said to his minister: "Your best work in the pulpit is when you put heart into people for the coming week." This is the other dimension necessary to our mission as true servants. Is our doing and being so closely identified, as Emil Brunner put it, that when a person turns to God desiring to serve him, God directs his attention to the world and its need?"

All this brings us to Isaiah's notion of our qualifications for effective service.

1. First of all, *what the servant says and does depends for its effect upon whom he or she is.* Behind the action, there must be a *life*. The servant in his or her service must in their doing be a witness to something spiritually unique in their

Lent and Easter

life. Someone once said: "Technicians are made; genius is inspired." The classroom or laboratory can produce a person whose performance is technically perfect, but someone who is adept at doing may not ever inspire others, especially the weary, to go on.

A minister, for example, may visit a sick room in the hospital, read a few verses from Scripture, pray a few stock sentences, and leave, but the result is if he or she had never been there. But perhaps someone else comes by, not even a learned person, and as he or she enters, the whole room lights up. This is an inner gift, not learned from books, but is a rare combination of being and doing. And it prompts every servant to ask: Am I gentle, kind and truly sympathetic? Do I say the right word at the right time in the right way? A stranger on a New York city bus turned to me and asked, "Are you saved?" That kind of service at the wrong time in the wrong place deserves to be ignored.

2. Another thought: How do we acquire this attitude, this combination of serving and witness? Isaiah lays his finger on it in verse 4 by "listening to God." *None of us can minister to the weary unless we bring a word or message that is bigger than ourselves.* Those who fail in this are simply not listeners. A pastoral call that consists of idle talk about little items does not move beyond the limits of our brain; it reaches no depth in the human soul. Isaiah showed his people a better way; those exiles for whom life had been a steady drag needed the face and touch of someone with a plus side to the business of living. You see: a prophet is not just a "foreteller," i.e., someone who predicts the future. The true prophet is a "forthteller," one who tells people what is God's will for them in their present situation. For this he himself must be a learner (v. 4b) and what he learns from God, he passes on to those in need. A woman was asked one day why she went to hear a certain preacher on Sundays and she replied simply, "He helps me." That is serving and witnessing of the highest and best order.

Palms and Thorns

3. A final point: *Such service is never easy.* Isaiah cautions us from his own understanding of the servant's mission. It demands determination and a special brand of stick-to-it-iveness. The servant's pilgrimage stirs adverse feelings in others. He wrote: "I gave my back to the smiters." (v. 6) Yet he sees the servant setting his "face like a flint," knowing his cause was good and the need to witness before the unfortunate was a necessity. Only in this way would every servant galvanize in others a sense of mission for their sake and the prospect of a better life for all.

Interestingly enough, we hear an echo of this principle in the words of Jesus: "Come unto me, all who labor and are heavy-laden, and I will give you rest. Take my yoke upon you and learn from me; for I am gentle and lowly in heart, and you will find rest for your souls." (Matthew 11:28, 29 RSV) Christianity, in keeping with its founder, is always turned to the future, but at the same time it reaches back to gather up those who are falling by the wayside; those whom the world has left behind. Doing what they do, Christians show what they are, and such a witness gives meaning to every life they touch. As one theologian said, "God came to us in the Redeemer so that we, learning from him, might go on redeeming others in his Name." And every day in some places and at some times, this way of life is vindicated by the impact and influence of God's servants upon those who are seeking for the right way.

---

[1] Quoted in *Concise Dictionary of Religious Quotations,* ed. by Wm. Neil (Grand Rapids, MI: Wm. B. Eerdmans, 1974), p. 148.

Servant Worship

Maundy Thursday *Psalm 116:12-19*

The season of Lent is drawing now to a close. On Ash Wednesday we said that Lent is not primarily a period when we "don't do this" or "don't do that"; rather it is intended to be a time of self-denial and self-discipline during which we tone up the moral fiber of our inner being and when we place greater emphasis upon the spiritual and less upon the material. As someone has said, "It is a matter of adding as well as subtracting." If we have been serious at all, our aim during the past few weeks should have been our taking second place to our independence as persons and giving God and his presence greater priority in our daily lives. In so thinking and doing we would have been probably more honest with ourselves and in our moments of quiet devotion have asked seriously whether or not life has really any meaning in this topsy-turvy world.

Our attention today is upon the 116th Psalm, which combines elements of true worship, namely, thanksgiving to God, with the love of service which that worship induces and inspires. Note how the Psalm begins: "I love the Lord *because*

Palms and Thorns

. . . ." (v. 1) Then follows a list of what John Newton, the hymnwriter, called the "many dangers, toils and snares" that the Psalmist had coped with and the spiritual depths from which he had been drawn. His journey, like ours, had been within a real world, marked by affliction, fear, and even a brush with death, yet by God's amazing grace he came through, and the experience taught him the deeper meaning of a strong personal relationship with God and how it emerged finally in a life of endless gratitude and praise.

What concerned the Psalmist now was this persistent question: How can I ever repay God? In light of all these benefits and blessings, what can I be or do to even up the score? Note the three steps he took:

1. *"I will take . . . ." (v. 13a)* This is the best way to thank God. What God wants us to do in view of his love for us is simply to receive it. We begin to repay God by accepting willingly what he gives, that is, what he has done and will go on doing for us. We are empty. Therefore, to be what he wants us to be and to have what he wants us to have, we must open ourselves to his love in our lives. Only in this way are we able to carry out his will for us. And that love is most happy when it sees its reflection in the person who receives it. The Gospel writer said, ". . . there will be more joy in heaven over one sinner who repents than over ninety-nine righteous persons who need no repentance." (Luke 15:7 RSV)

It is true that our Christian worship involves giving, but more important in the eyes of God is our taking. God's love and grace are already here and they are his free gift to us. Our offertory response says:

> *All things come of thee, O Lord,*
> *And of thine own have we given thee.*

We repay God by taking, because we have nothing which is not already his. Here, before us, are the sacramental

Lent and Easter

symbols of bread and wine. As we take them into ourselves, our action should mean and signify that inwardly we will resolve to make God's love and will the guiding and molding factors in our common life.

    2. The Psalmist takes a second step: *"I will call . . . ."* *(v. 13b)* There is nothing unusual in calling God's name. People do it every hour of every day, sometimes in blasphemy, sometimes in defiance, and sometimes in utter faithlessness. But note how the Psalmist puts it: "I will call *on* the name of the Lord." By this he meant two-way communication with God. And the highest form of such a dialog is prayer. A theologian once said, "Prayer is our way of talking with God" and another wrote, "Our lifeline with and to God is maintained through the discipline of prayer." Paul Lehmann, in an address before Princeton students, declared: "Prayer is that meeting with God and man in which each is exposed to the other as he is." God's nature is known to us — as it was to the Psalmist — in all he has given us and hence his integrity is not at stake. But our integrity is, because what we pray and how we pray tells us what we are. John Kelman said in one of his sermons, "It will generally be found that a man's most distinguishing feature lies in the thing for which he has most frequently prayed."[1] If we are sincere as persons and honest in our requests, we open windows and doors so God can get to us. Then something can happen. However, it is always easier to organize our lives around ourselves and attempt daily to bend others to our own will, even God. We try to mold his will to ours instead of bending ours to his. But the Psalmist called the name of the Lord, i.e., he called God in upon his human situation, and in so doing he would help to bring about the answer to his prayers.

    He said, moreover, that he would perform his devotion "in the presence of all his people." (v. 14b) This is what we Christians mean and do when we say, *"Our* Father." None of us should ever feel we are the only ones who pray or

Palms and Thorns

know how to pray. Behind us are the Christians of all the ages past (what the writer to the Hebrews called "a cloud of witnesses" 12:1) and we are heirs of their faith and devotion. When we call upon God in prayer, we are part of a great fellowship who share together in both receiving and giving.

3. The third step the Psalmist took was: *I will offer . . . ." (v. 17)* In view of what he has been given and what he has been able to talk, the Psalmist says, "I will offer to thee the sacrifice of thanksgiving." (v. 17b) Someone will say, "O, that's easy! We do that every day." Of course, a routine "Thank you very much" is easy, and often when we thank God we do so "trippingly of the tongue." But the Psalmist's idea of thanksgiving was much, much more: it had in it the element of sacrifice. True, he remembered what God had done for him and he, like us, could name the beauty of the earth, the glory of the seasons, the food and clothing we take for granted, and so on. But the Psalmist's thanksgiving was basically for whom and what God is. And when we thank God for that, it is not entirely complete until what God is is claimed by us and invited to become the essence of our way of life. Whatever else God is, he is love. And when the Paslmist says "I love the Lord because . . ." (v. 1), it means that God's love displaces in the Psalmist all traces of self-love, and certainly this means sacrifice. To repay God for his love and blessings in this way, the believer subordinates his life to God's will and purpose. And this is costly.

Love so amazing, so divine,
Demands my soul, my life, my all.
(Isaac Watts, 1674-1748)

---

[1]Quoted by R. J. Wedderspoon in "Intercession" in *Expository Times,* LVII, 1, p. 20)

The Vicarious Servant

Good Friday   *Isaiah 52:13—53:12*

The beloved English cleric, Geoffrey Studdert Kennedy, wrote a poem, titled *The Unutterable Beauty*, which makes appropriate hearing on Good Friday:

> *When Jesus came to Golgotha, they hanged him to*
>   *a tree;*
> *They drove great nails in hands and feet and made*
>   *a Calvary.*
> *They placed on him a crown of thorns; red were his*
>   *wounds and deep,*
> *For those were crude and cruel days, and human*
>   *flesh was cheap.*
>
> *When Jesus came to Birmingham, they simply passed*
>   *him by;*
> *They never hurt a hair of him; they only let him die.*
> *For men had grown more tender and they would not*
>   *give him pain;*
> *They only just passed down the street and left him*
>   *in the rain.*

Palms and Thorns

> *Still Jesus cried, "Forgive them for they know not what they do,"*
> *And still it rained the wintry rain that drenched him through and through.*
> *The crowds went home and left the streets without a soul to see,*
> *And Jesus crouched against a wall and cried for Calvary.*[1]

Today is observed throughout the Christian world as Good Friday (sometimes known in earlier years as "God's Friday") and one can safely claim it to be probably the most solemn day of the Church Year. By the same token, our scripture lesson today is certainly one of the greatest religious writings of all time in its relevance, lofty literary style and deep spiritual sentiment and devotion. Some persons among us may never have read it, but many remember those familiar lines in the aria and chorus of Handel's *Messiah:* "He was despised and rejected of men; a man of sorrows and acquainted with grief . . ." and "All we like sheep have gone astray." (vv. 3, 6 KJV) Scholars have debated through the centuries over the identification of the person or persons referred to in this chapter; some have said it is the people of Israel, others the prophet himself, and Christ. Joseph Parker, who would be labelled today as representative of the "old school," once pointed out that of all the great persons of all the leading religions of the world, none matches the profile and portrait of this chapter, except Christ.

What is significant for us now, however, is not so much the identification of the servant as it is the spiritual principle at the heart of it, a principle which determines and shapes the character and mission of the servant; namely, the example of the dedicated person giving himself for the many so that the goodness and truth in his life might be realized in them. In the summer of 1941, when the German *Luftwaffe*

Lent and Easter

rained death from the skies over England's cities and towns, the Royal Air Force was perilously outnumbered, yet with courage beyond measure and at enormous sacrifice they engaged the enemy and won. This led Winston Churchill to declare: "Never in the realm of human conflict was so much owed by so many to so few." Here is the principle defined tersely in terms of the secular realm. In the realm of the Christian enterprise and mission, however, it means for you and me as servants of Christ to reach out and witness at whatever cost, so that the Christ in us may be formed and realized in others. St. Paul wrote in his Letter to the Galatians: "My little children, with whom I am again in travail until Christ be formed in you!" (4:19)

Over against the Christ figure here is set the rather shameful performance of humankind in which even to this day you and I are not free from blame. Note these lines: "As one from whom men hide their faces he was despised . . . We have turned every one to his own way." (vv. 3, 6) Do these words not alert our attention to one of the most prevalent of our human faults today, namely, indifference? Are we so busy serving ourselves that we lack any sensitive concern for the sorry plight of others? The homeless? The unemployed? The handicapped? The drug addicts? The good people whose lives have tumbled in? Is our expression, "I'm sorry," merely a polite exchange? Do we dismiss it all with a wave or a shrug, saying: "That's the way the cookie crumbles"? Are we like some bystanders at Calvary of whom it was written, "And sitting down they watched him there." (Matthew 27:36 KJV) How appropriate is that ancient cry from the city of Jerusalem in its moment of desolation and forsakenness: "Is it nothing to you, all you who pass by?" (Lamentations 1:12 RSV)

Perhaps there is something you and I can do in order to reverse this human attitude and make a world of difference in these times of suffering and crying needs.

Palms and Thorns

1. The first thing we can do is to turn sympathy *for* into sympathy *with*. Sympathy *for* is the attitude of the Priest and Levite on the Jericho Road who looked upon the robbed and beaten man in the ditch, then "passed by on the other side." Sympathy *with* shows the Samaritan getting off his donkey and ministering to a wounded brother in need of help. He bridged the distance between himself and an inconvenience which the others dismissed through sheer indifference.

Sympathy *for* fails to become sympathy *with* as long as we know little about each other and care less. Everywhere human hearts crave for sympathy. How few of us are like the prophet Ezekiel who said, "I sat where they sat." How many there are around us who seemingly are saying: If only someone would come out of the careless crowd and let us feel we have the sympathy of at least another human heart!

Jesus always bridged the distance between those on the wayside and those on the way. He was ever passing by, but how keen were his eyes for those in need. And every need that met his eyes touches his heart. "For the Son of man also came not to be served but to serve, and to give his life as a ransom for many," (Mark 10:45 RSV) he said to his disciples. His was sympathy *with*, and only as we catch his spirit will our indifference be put down. A Roman Catholic cleric agreed to leave an affluent assignment in the South to assume leadership in a popular diocese in the North where social problems of every sort abounded. Someone asked him "Why?" and he replied, "I see Jesus Christ in the face of the poor."

2. This leads us to a second thought: *We must become more sensitive to the effects of sin.* One day a man went into a small shop that specialized in religious souvenirs and similar mementos. He asked the clerk if she had any small silver crosses. "Yes," she replied, "but do you want a plain one or one of those with the little man on it?"

Lent and Easter

Some years ago while fulfilling an engagement at St. Olaf's College in Northfield, Minnesota, I was invited to visit a small room in the library where there was a display of many miniature crosses made by one member of the faculty. Along with the group of visitors was the distinguished Roman Catholic Cardinal Willebrands of the Netherlands who paused before a crucifix, that is, a cross with the model of the body of Jesus on it. He pointed out to me that the empty cross of the Protestant tradition fails to etch upon our imagination the enormity of sin that could put to death the perfect Son of God.

Certainly the Cardinal had a point. The Protestant symbol of the cross encircled with the victorious crown declares Christ's victory, but the suffering Savior on "the old rugged cross" is a necessary part of the picture; it is the prelude to victory and it never allows us to lose sight of the stark sinfulness of sin. And neither does the prophet when he wrote: "He was wounded for our transgressions; he was bruised for our iniquities; upon him was the chastisement that made us whole, and with his stripes we are healed." (v. 5) Before a spiritual reality as strong as that, can any one of us remain ambivalent or indifferent any longer?

3. Then, a final thought: Good Friday is a day of remembrance, but it is also a *moment for decision.* As we "survey the wondrous cross," we can be like those on that awful day at Calvary — enemies, indifferent grumblers, idle watchers — merely passersby. Or, we may join that little company of those who cared. Surely they had sympathy with him and were pierced to the heart by the callousness of human sin. But as they went away from the hill and into the world of their time, they were to become witnesses to a new life bought for them by him. And as they carried the Gospel into a hostile and indifferent future, Christ would see — as the prophet wrote — "the fruit of the travail of his soul and

Palms and Thorns

be satisfied." (v. 11) Shall we let them down? Cecil Alexander's lines are our answer:

> *O dearly, dearly has he loved,*
>   *And we must love him too;*
>   *And trust in his redeeming blood*
> *And try his works to do.*
>   *(1823-1895)*

---

[1]Quoted by William Purcell in *Woodbine Willie: A Biography of Studdert Kennedy* (London: Hodder & Stoughton, 1962), pp. 211-212.

The Outcome of Easter Faith

The Resurrection of Our Lord　　　　　*Isaiah 25:6-9*

Carl Hopkins Elmore once told of a Jewish rabbi who was so moved and disturbed by the maltreatment of his race in certain sections of the world that he sent this appeal to all Christendom on the eve of another Easter:

> *I challenge the Christian world to measure itself by the standards of Christ. As long as any group is judged by its creed or color or country in place of its character, Christianity is a sacrilege rather than a sanctity. To this end I summon Christians everywhere to make this Easter to signify Christ* realized *and not merely Christ risen.*[1]

Are not the words of our text a declaration of judgment over against the situation Dr. Elmore describes? To read these Scripture verses thoughtfully is to be struck by how strong and accurate is his indictment of an attitude of mind and heart toward Easter that is all too common among Christians today. Many of us, even church members, will greet

Palms and Thorns

Easter morning with the triumphant strains of "Christ the Lord is Risen Today!" but will pass over the world-shaking implications of this fact unacknowledged and unexplored. It means no more to them than that history records one Jesus of Nazareth who lived and died sometime between 4 B.C. and A.D. 33 and whose memory time has not been able to flout or destroy. At best, Easter is a delightful festival and provides a pious note to harbinger the coming of spring.

Does not this situation and frame of mind cast a shadow over what we think and do on Easter Day? Indeed, it makes sharply apparent to us that the face of Christ risen is not enough. And it will never be enough until we turn a first-century fact into a living twentieth-century reality, namely, Christ realized in our daily lives. Isaiah talks about a God who has defeated death, who saves his people, and in whom all should rejoice and be glad. And our crowded churches on this Easter Day prove that at least we acknowledged what God has done. But here is where many of us stop short. The writer of the First Epistle of Peter refers to something more. He says: "As the outcome of your faith you obtain the salvation of your souls. (1:9 RSV) This is Christ realized! And unless we face up to this challenge and its claim upon our devotion and worship, we shall miss the true benefit and blessing of this Easter Day.

1. Our first step, then, is to recognize that *a true celebration of Easter is possible only if we pay a price.* None of us should come to Easter Day light-heartedly with bunnies, blossoms and the chirping birds of spring. Peer Gynt, in Henrik Ibsen's play by the same name, had just listened to a soft and harmless sermon at the funeral of a man with a wretched reputation, and he came away, saying: "There was nothing in it to make us feel uneasy."

And this is the tragic weakness of so much of our Easter worship. It is merely a matter of giving assent to the fact of one risen from the dead, but it is not a matter of real

Lent and Easter

belief. It is perilously easy to come to church once a year in such numbers as crowd our sanctuaries on this day and to sing with superficial enthusiasm, "Now above the sky he's King!" But if our Christian faith were vital and real, we should be frantically impatient until the Risen Christ were realized in every area of our lives. We salute a fact — that is easy; but are we able to rejoice meaningfully and intelligently over the reality of salvation? If not, there ought to be something here "to make us feel uneasy." Effort and cost are involved. Christ risen — that entailed a price paid by God. Christ realized — that is the price to be paid by you and me.

Easter Day is certainly an occasion to rejoice. But over what? It is simply the prospect of our living forever? Because Jesus once said, "Because I live you will live also," (John 14:19 RSV) do we presume that this is automatically going to happen? If so, we are overlooking the fact that Christ's aliveness was secured by the bloody sweat of Gethsemane and a ghastly and ignominious death upon Calvary. Indeed, no one of us has any right to celebrate or share in the victory of Easter Day who has not been through a Good Friday experience in which we have broken down all our worldly priorities and thrown ourselves upon the mercy of Christ, saying: "Nothing in my hand, I bring/Simply to thy Cross I cling." And that same Christ confronts us still today with the solemn and serious question: "Are you able to drink of the cup I drink of?" (Matthew 20:22 RSV)

2. Then, a second step is to realize that *the outcome of our Easter faith depends upon how genuine is our commitment to the Risen Christ.* To grant the fact that Christ is risen, we said, is a comparatively easy thing, but Christ realized is far more difficult because the quality and integrity of our surrender to him are involved. In the New Testament the central message of the preaching of the apostles was "this Jesus whom God raised up whereof we are witnesses." (Acts 2:32 RSV) And the amazing success of their preaching came from

Palms and Thorns

an experience of the Risen Christ in their souls. Each had come face-to-face with him. In spite of threats of torture and death, each of them had decided for Christ. Each of them knew — as someone said — "that intensely personal experience by which a man is turned inside out, his world upside down, and heaven right side up." Moreover, each of them knew that through every storm and pain and tragedy the Risen Christ would hold them fast — if they would let him.

> *One day in the Alps, a mountain climber and his guide came to a dangerous chasm which dropped away hundreds of feet into a rough and jagged gorge. The only way to get across safely was for the traveller to place his foot into the outstretched hand of the guide who could place it on* terra firma *on the other side. But the climber hestitated and drew back. The guide, sensing his terror, shouted back to him a word of reassurance, "Don't worry! This hand has never lost a man!"*

You see, it comes down finally to this question: What is Easter in the pattern of your experience and mine? Just another acknowledgment of Christ risen? Or, is it the proof of the commitment of your life to Another Life so that his purpose, goodness, and love are seen and realized in you? This requires an Easter Faith that is first-hand and vital. And its object is trustworthy. The strong arm with its nail print has never lost a man.[2]

---

[1]*The Inexhaustible Christ* (New York: Harper & Brothers, 1935), p. 121.

[2]Some of the ideas in this sermon are from the author's own volume, *Higher Reaches* (London: Epworth Press, 1970), pp. 126-131.

Beginning with Easter — Then What?

Easter 2   *Acts 4:32-37*

How often have we heard this remark: "What can you do for an encore?" Or, "That's a hard act to follow!" Easter Day is now behind us: we've sung the great Alleluias, chanted hymns of victory, and put the blossoms and lilies on a sunny windowsill. But what of it all? Is it now a closed event? Or, more appropriately: Is it just the beginning? Charles Wesley in his Easter hymn sang: "Love's redeeming work is done." How can we follow that act? Can there be an encore? This is exactly where you and I come in.

Look for a moment at the scenes that followed upon the first Easter Day. The disciples, we are told, had been in hiding, fearing the enemies of Jesus, but it must be noted that they were meeting as a little company to meditate and pray. Then came the rousing experience of Pentecost and we learn that these fearful and cowering disciples became persons of strength and courage who burst upon the world with a message of new life through a Risen Lord. Extraordinary things began to happen: conversions occurred; lame and ailing people were healed; Peter and John, though arrested

Palms and Thorns

by vengeful civic authorities, stood up resolutely against them; and little companies of spiritually reborn persons testified to the strange and wonderful presence in their midst of the living Lord. Listen to Luke's account: "And when they had prayed, the place in which they were gathered together was shaken; and they were all filled with the Holy Spirit and spoke the word of God with boldness." (Acts 4:31 RSV)

If this was not an encore, whatever else could it be? The aftermath, then, of that first Easter provides a model for us in the Christian church today. And as we explore what occurred we discover what are really our spiritual needs and the key to their solution.

1. *In the Easter experience is found the key to genuine community.* This sense of community grew out of a peculiar fellowship quite unlike any religious phenomenon before or since. Certainly there were other groups and agencies at work in the world of their time: civic government was intact; philosophers were clustered as Stoics or Epicureans; commercial leaders got together over trade; and the result was a society in which organization was the key to certain ends. But these disciples and their friends were different. Others worked from the outside in order to create an "in" group, consisting of persons who qualified socially, academically or economically to belong. The Christian group, however, came together as a result of a new power. They were people who had had a common experience of the life and spirit of Jesus of Nazareth and they met to talk and pray about what his death and resurrection really meant. They witnessed before one another to the presence in their lives of the Risen Christ and to the impact and effectiveness of this fact upon their lives. (v. 33) And as they did so within the confines of their little groups, they felt power coming into them, a power which united them in spirit and sent them out to witness before the world as the genesis and essence of a new community.

Lent and Easter

2. This new sense of community, however, was no emotional "flash in the pan." *It emerged in action and that action became the mission of the early church.* Here we see two movements: one spiritual, the other social. And the latter grew out of and was shaped by the former. As Joseph Parker said from his London pulpit: "The hand cannot go without the heart." Moreover, the heart cannot go without a higher spiritual bidding. In keeping with these facts this group embarked upon a new mission. They became a community of sharing, caring, helping persons, freed from human selfishness and the narrowness of personal ambition. All these things came automatically because inwardly they decided that if God be God and if it was true that he revealed himself supremely in the love and power of Jesus Christ, then great things were bound to happen to them who believed. Theirs was like the resolve of Martin Luther King, Jr., when he received the Nobel Prize in Norway, and said: "It's a commission to go out and work harder for the things in which we believe."

Does not all this have something to say about our Easter worship and its integrity? If Sunday worship is considered to be merely something to make us feel better, a sort of limited therapeutic, then it is just a fruitless episode. But if we come to church to witness joyfully to the victories of the past week, the occasions when your Christian faith worked, sustained and held you fast, then we have a mission to go back out into the world with ourselves as examples of a new way of life that nothing can underrate or destroy.

3. A further post-Easter lesson comes to us from our scripture passage of today: we see the key to true leadership. *To decide to act is useless without the will to carry it out.* This lack of strong will is the reason for the lack of worthy leadership in our modern society. Luke rounds out this paragraph with the personal example of the disciple called Barnabas. Listen to this case study in verses 36-37: "Barnabas

Palms and Thorns

... sold a field which belonged to him and came and laid it at the apostles' feet." You and I cannot divorce or separate the Easter experience from stewardship. Those who commit themselves to others, to things great and good, become not only worthy examples but automatically they become leaders in causes that change our world. Billy Graham asked President Bok of Harvard, "What is the biggest thing that is missing among students on your campus today?" And Bok answered in one word: "Commitment." Barnabas by his sincere commitment channeled the aims, efforts and convictions of others into the work of the Kingdom. Renan once remarked that, "Christianity has done Barnabas an injustice in not placing him foremost among the apostles." He raised the curtain upon the Easter encore. It is ours to do, too, if we would only have the will to join him.

Passing the Easter Miracle On

Easter 3   *Acts 3:13-15, 17-19*

Three short illustrations fit aptly into the pattern of our thinking today:

1. Mark Antony, in his eulogy at the funeral of Julius Caesar, had just whipped up the emotions of the crowd to fever pitch, and as they broke out into a vengeful mob seeking Brutus and the other traitors, Antony stood by and remarked: "There let it work!"

2. A visitor to the City of Rome was being shown the wealth and riches of the Roman Church — its monuments, shrines, gilded altars and diamond studded chalices — and the guide remarked to him, "No longer can it be said of the church, 'Silver and gold have I none.' " "True," said the visitor, "and neither can the church say to the lame man at the gate, 'In the name of Jesus of Nazareth, rise up and walk.' "

3. A minister had taken his young son on a tour of a great locomotive plant where at that time huge steam engines were

being made for the nation's railroads. They stood almost in awe before a large sixteen-wheeler which was belching steam from its tubes and valves. The minister remarked to the boy, "Doesn't this enormous bulk of power remind you of our church?" "Yes, in a way," said his son, "but it moves!"

Here in this third chapter of the Book of Acts, Luke presents one of those scenarios so typical of the early post-Easter days. Peter and John are seen going up to the Temple at the hour of prayer. Already past and over was the ecstatic experience of the Day of Pentecost, yet they continued the regular Hebrew discipline of a daily rendezvous with God. On their way in, they met a lame man, a cripple from his birth, who had been carried there by his friends and laid at the gate where he might beg for coins from passersby. Hundreds had passed him through the years, but no one had ever cured him; indeed many did not give him as much as a glance. But Peter stopped and, looking at him, said: "Look on us! Silver and gold have I none, but what I have I give to you." (v. 6) What did he have? Something unique: inner power, a blessing from a deep spiritual experience, the result of an encounter with the reality of a Living Lord. "In the name of Jesus Christ of Nazareth, walk," said Peter, and the man rose up with strong feet and ankles and entered the Temple with them "walking and leaping and praising God." (vv. 7-8)

What an astounding sight this must have been for those standing by. Indeed, they were dumbfounded to say the least — and rightly so! Wouldn't you and I have been so, too? And would we not, like them, be eager to know what was behind this tremendous event? Peter, however, knowing these people and their belief in magic and superstition, hastened to forestall any such notion, saying: "Why do you wonder at this and why do you stare at us, as though by our own power or piety we had made him walk?" (v. 12) It was not, then,

Lent and Easter

a matter of magic or a sleight of hand trick intended to excite their wonder for a moment and then fade out almost instantly. It was a genuine miracle and as such it had a past, present and future which gives it a lively credibility even to this day.

1. First of all, there was the past element: *the miracle of Peter himself.* For us to read the final chapters of the synoptic Gospels and the first chapters of the Book of Acts is to feel there were two Peters: the one before the Resurrection and the one afterwards. Who would recognize these as the same man? During Jesus' ministry Peter was a clumsy, blundering fisherman, always asking the wrong questions and protesting the truth in order to save his own hide. Nothing less than a miracle can account for this new Peter after the Resurrection. And the test of this lies in the fact that you cannot work a miracle unless you yourself are a miracle. The lame man owed his cure to someone else's faith, but Peter gave only what he himself had already received. ("I give you what I have." v. 6) A politician once said about his rival: "That man will go far because he believes every word he says." You see, such belief is always contagious; it is caught from another's convictions. Peter was a witness to the Resurrection (note how often he said, "God raised [him] from the dead. To this we are witnesses," 3:15) and this sealed forever his faith in Christ. So, for this lame man, Peter was the medium through whom the effect of the miracle of a Risen Lord flowed and the result was that, as Luke put it, "The name of Jesus, by awakening faith, has strengthened this man, whom you see and know, and this faith has made him completely well." (3:16 NEB)

2. This leads us to the second element in the miracle: *the present power in Jesus' name.* For us, in our time, a name can be just a label for routine identification. We choose names for our children sometimes for odd reasons. Biblically, however, having a name told a story: it summed up a person's

Palms and Thorns

character. As someone said, in the Bible a name was "a condensed definition." Or, as Albert C. Winn wrote: "[A name] stands in a very real way for the man himself. All his authority, all his power, all his essential self, are caught up in his name."[1]

Do we realize, then, what we mean when we use the phrase, "in Jesus' name"? The hymn writer, Caroline Noel, sang, "At the name of Jesus, Every knee shall bow." Why? Because every true Christian believes it is through his name that we are saved. Do you know how the first Christians identified themselves to one another? They were, as you are well aware, an "endangered species." They were constantly in peril of their lives. Hence they drew in the sand a symbol in the shape of a fish. Why a fish? Because in the Greek word for fish each of the letters stood for a word key to their beliefs, "Jesus Christ, God's Son, Savior." "Jesus" (his humanity); "Christ" (the climax of revelation); "God's Son" (his divinity); "Savior" — all these together signified our salvation through his name. And all through succeeding ages, whenever and wherever ordinary people surrendered to him and put their faith in his saving power, miracles occurred: sinful persons found new freedom from their ugly pasts; unbelieving wanderers were re-born into new life; and weak and fearful mortals received a strange new power that made them into instruments for freedom, justice and good will everywhere on earth.

3. We come now to the third element in the miracle: the people implement this faith in *the future mission of the church.*

Peter had testified before these people to his own faith in the Risen Christ. The lame man was evidence of that healing faith impacting upon another's life. But what about the whole company of curious folk who had watched the miracle occur? Listen to what Peter said to them: "Repent, then, and turn to God, so that he will wipe away your sins ... and that he may send Jesus who is the Messiah .... You must

Lent and Easter

listen to everything he tells you." (3:19, 22 TEV) To use a slang phrase, Peter had now "tossed the ball into their court" and seemingly said in Marc Antony's phrase, "There let it work!" Will the outcome of the miracle — in the words of the Scottish lad — will it "move"? Or, will the church of the ages onwards be able by its faith to say: "In the name of Jesus of Nazareth, rise up and walk"? Peter would say, "Yes." But there was a catch in all this: they must repent and accept Christ as Savior and listen to what he had to say to them.

Now, you cannot repent fully and genuinely unless and until your conscience becomes sensitized to the nature and reality of human sin. And this brings us to the Cross and to a pivotal element in the atoning work of Christ. To look at the Cross is to see what sin could do to one who was the sinless Son of God, and to have our conscience stabbed awake is the beginning of repentance and of the redeeming work of Christ in our lives. The old Gospel hymn refrains:

Look, look, look and live,;
There is life for a look at the crucified One,
There is life in that moment for thee.

The miracle does not end there; it has a future in the world of common men and women. Jesus said to the disciples in his final appearance before them: "Go, therefore, and make disciples of all nations . . . ." (Matthew 28:19 RSV) But note that what he said before this command: "All power in heaven and on earth has been given to me." "Therefore" they were to launch his mission through his church and into the world. They were to become allies with his risen power and through faith in its reality they would become his instruments in the fulfilling of God's purpose for the salvation of humanity. Anything they could do for themselves paled into insignificance in the face of a challenge and price as great as this. Remember Sidney Carton at the close of Dickens' novel, *A Tale of Two Cities*, as he went to his death for the sake of his friend, how there echoed within him the triumphant words of Christ, "I am the resurrection and the life, saith the Lord. He that believeth in me though he die, yet shall he live; and he that liveth and believeth in me shall never die." And then there followed this magnificent affirmation:

> *I see the lives for which I lay down my life, peaceful, useful, prosperous, happy, in that England I shall see no more.... I see that I hold a sanctuary in their hearts, and in the generations hence.... It is a far, far better thing I do than I have ever done; it is a far, far better rest that I go to, than I have ever known.*

---

[1] *The Layman's Bible Commentary,* "The Acts of the Apostles" (Richmond, VA: John Knox, 1967), p. 44.

An Easter Dividend: The Courage To Be and To Do

Easter 4   Acts 4:5-13

In the year 1793 when the French armies were laying siege to the Mediterranean fortress of Toulon, Napoleon built a battery in such an exposed position that the other officers said he would never get a soldier to man it. But Napoleon set up beside it a large sign with these words, "The Battery of Men without Fear." And he was never at a loss for volunteers to man it.

Madame Chiang Kai-shek, wife of the one-time Head of State in China, was visiting America some decades ago and was invited to deliver the commencement address at Wesleyan College in Macon, Georgia. She closed her remarks with this little verse:

> *Life is mostly froth and bubbles;*
> *Only two things stand like stone:*
> *Kindness in another's troubles,*
> *Courage in your own.*

What quality do we most admire in another person? Certainly we admire ability of any and every kind — the ability to write a great book, to paint a splendid picture or to compose inspiring music. But over and above these abilities, the quality which never fails to excite our applause and admiration is courage. However, there are many kinds and levels of human courage, and it may be necessary for all of us to probe more deeply into its nature if we are to discover what creates the type most to be fostered and admired.

Once in a sermon in New York, the Reverend Charles E. Jefferson of the Broadway Tabernacle said:

> *The world is inexpressibly rich in courage. And at the same time the world is inexpressibly poor in courage. We are richly supplied with military courage, but we are deficient in civic courage. We can fight victoriously in the armor of Caesar, but we are awkward and often important in the armor of God. The whole world is waiting for the development of a higher form of courage.*[1]

I do not suppose there has ever been a time in our experience when there was more physical courage seen among the world's people than in these days — and by physical courage I mean sheer dogged ability to hold on — and we thank God for it. But what is tragically lacking and what is most needed in his hour is moral and spiritual courage: the courage of one's convictions, the courage to stand alone in the name of truth, the courage to follow the right wherever it leads, the courage to scorn mediocre and slap-dash politics (even in an election year), the courage to be ridiculed and scoffed at in defense of principles too high and too great to be flouted. For most of us it is easier to face actual danger by the dint of sheer physical courage than to face misunderstanding, criticism, unpopularity, coldness or loss of friendship. For these demands a higher, more difficult kind of courage is entailed, and this no one can afford to be without if he or she is to live life nobly and well.

Lent and Easter

Our scripture passage today presents one of those great acts of moral and scriptural courage so characteristic of the early church. A lame man at the Gate Beautiful of the Temple had been healed by Peter and there was awe and wonder among those who witnessed the miracle. The priests and Sadducees got wind of this and had the apostles thrown promptly into jail. The next morning they were hustled before Annas and Caiaphas (the same men who had part in Jesus' trials) and were asked by what power and in whose name they had created this unseemly sensation at the Temple. Peter immediately squared his shoulders and answered that it was done in the name of Jesus of Nazareth by whose power alone people are saved. This courageous reply enraged the judges, but the ground was cut from under them when they saw the lame man, healed and strong, as evidence of the miracle that had occurred. So, they decided that discretion would be the better part of valor, and they ordered Peter and John to get out and to keep quiet about this Jesus of Nazareth. But the courage of these men was more than the officers had counted on and they were startled as Peter declared: "Whether it is right in the sight of God to listen to you rather than to God, you must judge; for we cannot but speak of what we have seen and heard." (v. 19 RSV)

That's courage! But it is more than ordinary courage — it is moral and spiritual courage. What else could explain the fact that Peter, a rude and unlearned peasant, who a few weeks before had run out on Jesus, was able to stagger the minds and authority of the civic rulers and high priests? What else could explain the fact that Peter, who had been unstable as water, was now a pillar of granite, defying and confounding the elite of "church and state" with a magnificent display of irresistible power of mind and heart and will? You see, real courage is moral and spiritual. It is not the absence of fear; it is the conquest of fear. It is not a physical endowment nor a matter of merely being built that way. To risk one's reputation for the sake of duty, "to stick to your guns" when public opinion is against you, to blaze a new trail when everyone else glides along the path of least resistance, requires a moral and spiritual quality that is gained only by moral and spiritual means. And if there is anything this generation must learn — and learn quickly — it is that the courage necessary to meet and change the world belongs to the realm of character and comes from the same sources that make people and nations great.

What, then, was the source of moral and spiritual courage that transformed Peter from a weakling into a bold advocate of the person and cause of Jesus Christ?

1. *Peter had encountered the risen Christ.* Peter was sure of his facts and that is why he was invincible. The secret of his Christian boldness was that he knew Jesus Christ was alive; he felt his presence within his soul, thrilling and inspiring and enlarging every thought and action of his life. What cared he then for the threats of any man or even the prospect of human danger? What could the world do to him when there reigned in his soul One who said, "Courage, I have overcome the world"? (John 16:33) What could even death do to him when his heart was throbbing with the power of the Master who had brought life and immortality to light?

We are told that one day in the first century a Christian was being tried before the Roman Governor, Pliny. "I will banish you," he roared at the poor creature who confronted him. "You can't," came the reply, "for the whole world is my Father's house." "I'll slay you," threatened Pliny. "You can't," said the Christian, "for my life is hid with Christ in God." "I will drive you away from everyone and you'll have not a single friend left," shrieked the Governor. "You can't," came the reply, "for I have a Friend from whom you cannot ever separate me!"

Now, whether or not we personally feel the need of moral and spiritual courage today, we must remember that our western civilization needs it desperately every hour. We must, therefore, by Bible reading, earnest prayer and regular worship and holy living, get closer to the Living Christ; so close that he becomes the soul of our soul, his will our will, and gradually there will arise in us that inner courage that will make us invincible. Each of us will then stand bravely for the right, in scorn of every consequence, because the Risen Christ has proved that the power of righteousness cannot be put down. And we shall live by the truth that the center and base of this universe is love, and even though the world nails it to a tree on Calvary, yet it cannot and will not die.

2. *Peter had begun to work for Jesus Christ.* Remember what happened after the Crucifixion? For Peter, John and the others the whole thing was a closed case, so they went back to their boats and nets by the Sea of Galilee. Then, you recall, Jesus came in the early hours of the dawn and called Peter, "Feed my sheep." And from that hour Peter threw himself so completely into the work and cause of Jesus that nothing could ever again shake him from it. From then on, he was gripped by the staunch conviction that the mission and fellowship of Jesus were the only things that mattered in all the world and that in giving himself one hundred percent to them, he was filled with the moral and spiritual courage to follow through to the end.

This same spirit was seen in the aged Polycarp when he was urged by the Roman government at Smyrna to curse Christ and so spare his own life. But the saintly figure replied: "Eighty-six years I have been his slave and he has done me no wrong. How can I blaspheme my King who saved me? Make me an anvil, Lord, smitten, but standing firm!"

3. *Peter knew that Jesus was counting on him.* No one ever hurt Jesus as much as Peter had done, and yet when he rose from the dead Jesus sent a special message to Peter that he still believed in him. The very fact that, human as we Christians are today and prone to failure, Jesus still counts on us

should give us a new determination and an inner spiritual courage to go on and never fail him.

There is an old legend which tells that after the Resurrection and Jesus had returned to heaven, an angel, seeing his wounds, said, "You must have suffered terribly for the people down there in the world." "Yes," said Jesus, "I did." "Do all people know how much you loved and suffered for them?" "No," replied Jesus, "as yet only a few in the corner of Palestine know the story." "Well," said the angel, "what have you done about letting everyone know about it?" Jesus said, "I have asked Peter and John and the others to tell others, and these others to tell still others until the farthest person on the widest circle has heard the story of it all." "But," continued the angel, "What if Peter and John forget? What if they fail in their task? Haven't you another plan?" And Jesus answered, "I have no other plan; *I am counting on them.*"

Let us put ourselves today in the place of Peter and John and realize that Jesus is still counting on us, too. Think of what this means! It means that we are part of his plan, that we are not meaningless nobodies upon the stage of human history, and as such are indispensable to him. His power and grace will always undergird you and me if we only accept them. Why, then, should we have any reason to be afraid?

---

[1]From an unpublished manuscript.

Easter Journeys Out and In

Easter 5 *Acts 8:26-40*

A local TV station has omitted the use of a commercial during one hourly break and has featured a spot announcement called *Reach Out*. It is a simple challenge to their viewers to reach out with all their affluence and resources to someone in need — the homeless, the friendless, the confused in mind and soul — and especially to bridge the gap between race and race, class and class, creed and creed.

A question can be raised appropriately: To what and with what? And any answer must work both ways. Any reaching out must be a mutual action. The person in need must reach out with his or her claims as fully as the person with answers and resources should do in their response. Only when the two meet in mutual acceptance will there be fullness of life for both.

No story excites the Christian mind to the degree that the miracle of the Resurrection does in its spread into the lands surrounding Jerusalem. Here, in these early chapters of the Book of Acts, is a recital of the activities and exploits of the early Apostles — Peter, John and Philip — as they went from town to town declaring the message of a Risen Lord and ministering to the sick, the crippled and those suffering from mental or spiritual miseries. Few of these anecdotes are more interesting than Philip's adventure into that lonely territory on the way south to the city of Gaza. He had already had a great time of it in the more populated centers of Samaria. Crowds were attracted to him and, as Luke put it, "gave heed to what was said by him" (8:6) and, moreover, "there was much joy" (v. 8) as a result of his visits among them. Then, strangely enough, he felt an inner compulsion to strike out into unknown territory in the direction of Gaza, one of the most southern cities on the main trade route to Egypt. And so we find him, a Jew, on a missionary venture into Gentile country.

Philip had not hiked very far when he was overtaken by a strange entourage, a caravan of wagons with footmen, captains and servants ahead and behind, with a single chariot whose passenger was reading aloud from a big scroll. Who was he? He was an Ethiopian (by the color of his skin), a cabinet minister to the Queen of Meroe in South Nubia, whose office controlled her royal treasury. The curious thing, however, was that he was a convert to Judaism who had made the long journey up to Jerusalem to worship in the Temple and on the return trip was reading the writings of the Old Testament prophet, Isaiah. What next? Why, Philip, with discreet apostolic boldness, accosted him and asked if he really understood what he was reading. The Ethiopian answered, "How can I, unless someone guides me?" Philip took it from there and hence we have this dramatic vignette portraying one of the earliest Christian conversions.

What shall we make of this incident? Is there anything in it really for us today? Certainly, and it is this: what happened on the Gaza road that day is a paradigm of the Christian process from encounter to confirmation. Let us take it step by step.

Lent and Easter

1. Verse 28: "Seated in his chariot, he was reading the prophet Isaiah." John Calvin cautioned us that ours must be an *informed* faith. It was in search of this that the Ethiopian was reading the Scriptures as he journeyed toward home. Is it not possible that after the experience of worship in Jerusalem he was asking himself: What is all this about? He was engaged in an exercise that many of us have failed to do, and we therefore are living a faith that makes little sense. It is exciting to be told that the United Bible Societies of the world distribute over 150 million copies of the Scripture every year. But the saddening question is: How many of these are actually read? In how many homes are the Scriptures shelved entirely out of reach and therefore out of mind? And what can be equally harmful is the manner in which the Bible is often read. Some read it merely for proof texts to underscore notions they already hold. Others who are narrow traditionalists read it with a closed mind and refuse to raise questions regarding points of view that are outdated or absurd. And some others pick up snatches of verses here and there with little connection before or after. But this Ethiopian was a reader of a different kind. He was an inquirer, and as such he was teachable. He was reading with a desire to know what was true. Philip asked him: "Do you understand what you are reading?" (v. 30)

2. And this leads us to the second step: the Ethiopian replied: "How can I, unless *someone guides me?*" (v. 33) Or, as the New English Bible puts it: "Unless someone will give me the clue." To read the Bible rapidly is of little use unless it is accompanied by true and honest understanding. Many of us approach the Bible as we would a recipe book, expecting to find and extract simple and concise solutions to our daily problems and troubles. This is a naive and fruitless exercise. The Ethiopian was not of this sort: "He invited Philip to come up and sit with him." (v. 33) And Philip explained to him the whole sweep of biblical revelation that climaxed in the coming of Jesus of Nazareth. (v. 35)

Palms and Thorns

Someone has said that the Bible tells us all we need to know about God, while Shakespeare shows us all we need to know about humanity. This is merely a half truth. The Bible tells us all we need to know about God *and* humanity. It is the story of the nature of God and his doings with humankind through the ages and of humankind's response to the unfolding of that drama throughout history. You and I will begin to understand the Scriptures when we see ourselves in this drama and are able to say about God in each story or crisis, "This is He" or "This is *me!*" It is then — and then only — that our reading of the Bible becomes most fruitful and productive in our common life. This is what Philip did for the Ethiopian. And the result?

3. This leads us now to step three: "And as they went along the road they came to some water, and the Ethiopian said, 'See, here is water! What is to prevent my being baptized?' "(v. 36) Not only was he teachable, but more important, he was *obedient.* He understood not only with the mind but also with the will. He raised no hurdles or made no excuses; he did not hedge and say he did not feel good enough to make this final decision. To do so would not be a sign of humility but of sheer dishonesty. He was ready to be baptized and this indicated that he understood.

Philip parted company with the Ethiopian, and we read that his new disciple "went on his way rejoicing." (v. 39) Why? Simply because he had found Christ. Moreover, he undoubtedly felt that on his return to his homeland he would never be bewildered any more, for now his life had new meaning and purpose and, even in the midst of heathen unbelief, he would know within himself a Presence that calms and satisfies every human heart.

Easter Turns
ONLY into ALSO

Easter 6   *Acts 10:44-48*

TWO simple yet rather apt incidents come to mind with regard to today's text:

1. A story comes from Cincinnati of a little Jewish boy who was told by his rabbi that he must no longer attend athletic classes in the Presbyterian gymnasium and swimming pool. Trying to explain this to the Presbyterian minister, who was much beloved for what he was doing for the boys of the community, the lad choked up and stammered, "Ain't religion hell?"

2. One hot day in Washington, a little African American boy was dangling his toes in the pool in front of the Lincoln Memorial on the Potomac. A passerby summoned a policeman and remonstrated that some kids today had no respect anymore. "I guess you're right," said the officer, but looking away from the frightened lad to the great statue of Lincoln, he added, "But somehow I feel it wouldn't have bothered *him* a bit."

Palms and Thorns

Two words in our American vocabulary are the key to many of our national and local problems. These words are: "prejudice" and "tolerance." And they are most controversial — and indeed relevant — when they figure in the field of religion. How frequently are we able to trace a rift in the church or community to human prejudice which someone once called "a lazy person's substitute for thinking." On the other hand, tolerance is one of the most lovable qualities any one of us can possess. It is the attitude that helps us see things from another's viewpoint and concedes others the right to their own opinions.

It is interesting to note how these two human attitudes were exercised and exerted early in the life of the Christian church. Their presence and the apostles' handling of the situations created thereby are made clear to us in the drama which our Scripture outlines for us today. A controversy arose from the encounter of the ancient Jewish religious tradition with the new understanding of faith and human integrity that the Gospel of the Risen Christ had brought. The religion of the Jews featured the word "only" (see Acts 11:19: ". . . preaching the word to none but unto the Jews only," KJV), while the message of the living Lord of Christianity was for others "also" (see Acts 10:45: "And the believers . . . were amazed because the gift of the Holy Spirit had been poured out even on the Gentiles," and Acts 11: ". . . the brethren who were in Judea heard that the Gentiles also had received the word of God." RSV) Easter had turned "only" into "also." Easter confronted Jewish exclusiveness with echoes of the words of Jesus: "I have other sheep that are not of this fold; I must bring them also, and they will heed my voice. So there shall be one flock, one shepherd." (John 10:16 RSV)

Let us review Luke's story in order to see clearly this turning point or the direction the early church took, without which Christianity would have remained merely a narrow Jewish sect within the borders of Palestine.

Lent and Easter

The drama begins with a significant person on stage, Cornelius, an officer of the Roman army, stationed in Caesarea, the capital of the provinces of Judea and Samaria. Daily he rubbed elbows with people of the Jewish faith and, surprisingly for a Roman, he had adopted some of the customs of their religion. Luke describes him in this way: "a devout man who feared God with all his household, gave alms liberally to the people, and prayed constantly to God." (Acts 10:2 RSV) One day, in his devotions, he had a strange vision in which a voice told him to send two emissaries to the town of Joppa, some distance south, and seek out a man named Peter who was stopping over with Simon, a tanner, in a house at the seaside. There was something almost revolutionary in this: Cornelius, a Gentile, would have ordinarily nothing short of contempt for Peter, a citizen of a race the Romans had conquered. But what was more, any Jew who consorted with a tanner was suspect, since Jewish law included strict prosecution against persons of this trade and would not allow them to set up shop within the official borders of any town. A Jewish rabbi once expressed this attitude in these words: "Woe unto that man who is a tanner." Nonetheless the messengers were sent.

Now we come to Act II. Peter had gone out that afternoon onto the rooftop of the tanner's house, and to the west he could see the shining waters of the Mediterranean Sea with the white sails of the boats and the larger cargo ships on their way to countries beyond the horizon. Suddenly, he was caught by a vision of a huge sheet let down from the heavens, laden with every sort of animal, reptile and bird anyone could imagine, and a voice said, "Rise, Peter, kill and eat." This occurred three times, and each time Peter protested on the basis of the ancient Jewish exclusiveness: "I have never eaten anything that is common or unclean." (v. 14) But the voice came back to him: "What God has cleansed, you must not call common." (v. 15) Just at this point the scene turns quickly to the arrival of the messengers with Cornelius' invitation.

The next day, the little company made off for Caesarea, where they found a group gathered in the house with Cornelius, who fell at Peter's feet. Peter made him rise, saying, "Stand up; I too am a man!" (v. 26) Then to the group he went on to say: "You know how unlawful it is for a Jew to associate with or visit anyone of another nation; but God has shown me that I should not call any man common or unclean." (v. 28) Hence, with this momentous breakthrough, the "only" of Judaism became the "also" of Christianity — and the result was memorable. "God shows no partiality," said Peter, "but in every nation anyone who fears him and does what is right is acceptable to him." (v. 35) Then, Luke tells us, "he commanded them to be baptized in the name of Jesus Christ." (v. 48)

Now let us come to Act III. The scene shifts to Peter in Jerusalem where he ran into a group of Jews who were upset by his new inclusiveness and thereby exposed their deep-seated prejudice. They nailed him immediately with a heated question: "Why did you go to uncircumcised men and eat with them?" No Gentile, in the eyes of these Jews, could be admitted into the fellowship of the early church by any other way than by the synagogue; in other words, they must first become Jews. Moreover, the further indiscretion adding insult to injury was that Peter had baptized them. Wow! But Peter held his ground and silenced them with these telling words: "If God gave the same gift to them as he gave to us when we believed in the Lord Jesus Christ, who was I that I could withstand God?" (11:17)

What of our day? Are the forces of tolerance fighting a losing battle against the stone wall of prejudice — in workshop, in school, in government and sadly in religion, too? What are the basics upon which true tolerance can be built from the Christian perspective?

Lent and Easter

1. *Christianity is an inclusive and never an exclusive faith.* Joseph Parker once remarked: "Jesus never came to make us less. He always comes to make us more." Christianity is a religion of enlargement. It excludes nobody. Listen to its language: "Whosoever will may come . . ." "Whosoever believes in him . . . ." It invites and lays its claim upon "all," "everyone," and "whosoever." And these words give the lie to every wrong interpretation of election. Often we hear questions raised about Jesus' words: "For many are called, but few are chosen," (Matthew 22:14 RSV) and the implication is that certain persons are favored while others are excluded from special acceptance. Election and chosenness are not exclusive. For example, the ancient Jewish law prescribed a seven-day week with six days for work and the seventh for rest. This did not mean that only the seventh was "God's day" and that the other six were beyond or outside his concern. It was found in practice that those who kept the seventh day holy were more inclined to keep the other six days accountable to God, too.

Or, take the Jewish people and their notion of chosenness throughout the whole of the Old Testament. This concept did not mean that all other people were destined to oblivion. As Christians, we owe much to the Jewish faith, but this does not mean we should be satisfied to stop with it rather than capture the best of it and claim this heritage for Christianity. As Christians, we do not draw a line of exclusion, for we are all children of God's grace, and though other religions may say, "You must come to us," Christianity comes to every human soul to seek and save them regardless of race, color or creed.

2. So far we have seen the new inclusiveness of Christianity at work, but we need now to ask: what was the basic reason or secret behind it all? What sustained the attitude and action of these early apostles and gave them the courage to be different? How do we explain this uncommon

Palms and Thorns

phenomenon — Jews and Gentiles, i.e., people divided by race, language and religion, joining in worship and eating meals together? *The answer lay in their common loyalty to Jesus Christ, their Risen and Living Lord.* Luke says, "In Antioch the disciples were for the first time called Christians." (11:26 RSV) These people acknowledged openly to one another that they belonged to Christ. Moreover, among the followers of Caesar and the paganism and immoralities of the cities of that day, they moved and lived as examples of goodness, not just refraining from evil but exercising positively a life of love. "Love one another as I have loved you" was their Master's command, and their strange loyalty to him broke the bonds of exclusiveness and fired their burning intention to win the world for him.

3. One further note must be made. Peter said *he was praying when the vision came.* (10:9, 30) The Westminster Shorter Catechism defines prayer as "an offering up of our desires unto God for things agreeable to his will." "Agreeable to his will" means openness on our part. The biblical question or cry from the seeking individual is always: "Lord, what will you have me to do?" Paul Tillich directs us to accept the fact that we are already accepted by God through Christ and that, therefore, all we need to do now is to allow the love that this fact affirms to emerge from us in attitude, word and deed. To live by the word "only" is to exclude others and to claim Christ as Savior for *me.* To live by the word "also" declares by our witness that he is Savior for *you,* too. John Wesley's words should become ours, too: "Give me your hand. I do not say, 'Come over to my side' or 'Draw me over to your side.' But if your heart be as my heart in the love of Christ, then give me your hand."

A Perspective on the Ascension

Ascension Day/Ascension Sunday   Acts 1:1-11

Today our focus is upon an unusual event which closed the earthly ministry of Jesus. Perhaps even more so than his Resurrection has the Ascension created unceasing controversy among believers and scholars alike. All four Gospels report Jesus' Resurrection in considerable detail, but it is only Mark and Luke who include the Ascension, albeit briefly. Luke, however, in this first chapter of *The Acts of the Apostles*, provides us with the fullest account in the New Testament.

Now, what about the Ascension? What interpretation can we put upon it in this age of doubt and ready skepticism? Or, what difference does it make whether or not we accept whatever truth lies in it?

First of all, let us look at what Luke tells us. After forty days of post-Resurrection appearances, Jesus had a final get-together with the disciples during which he cautioned them to remain in Jerusalem until the promise of the gift of the Holy Spirit would be realized. The disciples were confused — as they had been so often in his ministry — about the nature of the Kingdom. His answer, however, was: "You shall receive power when the Holy Spirit has come upon you; and you shall be my witnesses in Jerusalem and in all Judea and Samaria and to the end of the earth." (v. 8) Then "as they were looking on, he was lifted up and a cloud took him out of their sight." (v. 9) Moreover, as they gazed at this strange phenomenon, two men in white appeared beside them and asked an arresting question: "Men of Galilee, why do you stand looking into heaven? . . . This Jesus will come in the same way as you saw him go into heaven." (v. 11)

Here we have a reporter's eye-witness account. What do we make of it? Everything, as far as interpretation is concerned, will depend on our perspective or — as we say in America today — upon where you and I are "coming from."

a. There are, for example, the idealists. They take the story at face value. Jesus, in his earthly ministry, was a worker of miracles which were climaxed by the unprecedented miracle involving himself: resurrection from the dead. For forty days henceforward he would make appearances to his own followers and they would hear his familiar words, see the wounds in his body, and at times he would excite them with a sense of joy. Somehow, however, these phenomena had to end. Jesus had come from God and was given by God a mission to fulfill. All this was now accomplished and he could do no more than return to the God who sent him. So, the idealist says, "Case closed!"

b. A second perspective is that of the materialist. He takes a long, detached look at the whole story and dismisses it out of hand. To him it is an absurdity — just another myth. The early gospel writers had to dispose of Jesus somehow, and hence they wove this tale out of sheer fantasy. Moreover, the materialists ask: how could a human body of flesh and blood similar to ours simply go up into the air and disappear? They quote the first Russian astronaut who, upon his return to earth, declared he had had "up there" no intimations

Lent and Easter

of God. Moreover, even in every worshiping congregation today, you and I can see, here and there, the raised eyebrow or sense the armloads of questions: In this age of advanced science and cosmic exploration, doesn't the idea of an Ascension seem far, far out? Will he return like a space module and make a "re-entry"? Who are you kidding?

c. Perhaps the most helpful interpretation is that of the realist who looks at the whole incident from the perspective of the Christian believer. The more relevant question becomes then: How does the Ascension figure in one's own Christian experience? What is the *meaning* of the Ascension from this perspective for twentieth-century thinkers and believers? And is not that meaning clarified when we see the Ascension as an intermediate link between the Resurrection and the gift of the Spirit at Pentecost.

Let us now carry our thinking upon this event through three stages:

1. Luke tells us that *the Risen Lord charged the disciples to "wait." (v. 4)* What for? "The promises of the Father," he said. This can be a problem for many of us because we hate to wait. We have an aversion toward people who do not keep appointments on time, or trains and buses that arrive late, or postal systems that do not operate efficiently and so on. But these are secular problems with little moral orientation or content. The Bible, however, indicates something more when it tells us to wait. Waiting, for these disciples, was marked by reflection. Think of what they had been through during the past three years! They had been taught new views about life and religion. They had a new concept of God; no longer was he a stern and exacting law-giver, but a Father who loved his creatures, who was patient, long-suffering and kind. And in their Master they saw — as Leslie Weatherhead phrased it — all of God that could be poured into a solitary human being. Then came Calvary and their

whole world collapsed like a house of cards. But Easter Day dawned and they and the world were arrested by an unprecedented phenomenon, an unimagined surprise: Jesus arose, and for forty days he moved in and out among them, somehow but always wavering upon the frontier of two worlds. Was it possible there could be anything more? Yes, they were told to wait. And so the fearful little group met in secret, maintaining their personal commitment to Jesus, united in a spirit of expectation, and sharing in an attitude of openness to whatever the will of God had in store for them.

2. A second thought: *these waiting disciples were to experience the fulfillment of Jesus' promise — the gift of power. (vv. 4, 6, 8)* It was not, however, power in general or what we associate with social, intellectual, political or administrative achievement. It was power to be used for Christ and his Kingdom. Take Peter, for example. Look at the change this power wrought in his character. One moment he was declaring loyalty to Jesus; the next he was crying cowardly at a word from a housemaid. At one time his love for Jesus was at full tide; at another it had ebbed away. But now, in little more than a month, he became the recipient of power. Peter emerged from the period of waiting as a man of decision, of brave standing and of firm resolution. Like other early Christians, this disciple was to be described — as T. R. Glover put it — as one who "out-thought, out-lived, and out-died" the pagan world. This is what Jesus meant when he said he would send to his followers a Comforter, a word which means "strengthener." And whenever in the New Testament this spiritual power was given, it was for a purpose: that the work and mission of Christ would be carried on in and through his faithful followers. How can we get it today? We cannot get it; we can only wait to receive it. And when it comes, little companies of Christian men and women will form anew the phalanx of the church and face bravely a disbelieving world.

Lent and Easter

3. There is more — and this is where you and I are exposed to the real meaning and challenge of the Ascension story. *How is this power to be used?* Jesus spelled out the strategy of every Christian believer who asks: "Where do we go from here?" "You shall be my witness," he said, "in Jerusalem, Judea, and throughout the earth." This is a heady assignment because a true witness, even in our courts of law, has to report, not from heresay, but from a basis of "I was there." Moreover, that report must be given regardless of any personal cost and with the affirmation that it is "the truth, the whole truth, and nothing but the truth, so help me God"! So the apostles went out into the world with a message based upon personal experience of a Risen and Ascended Lord who for them had become "the way, the truth, and the life." Peter said to Annas, the high priest, at an early trial: "We cannot but speak of what we have seen and heard." (Acts 4:20 RSV) With this strange new power they set out from Jerusalem, their home base, and like concentric circles the Word went out under Christ's original command, "Go into all the world and preach the gospel to the whole creation." (Mark 16:15 RSV)

One thing more: the first Ascension story gives to us today in the church new meaning and significance to the words "waiting," "power" and "witness." It gives also to us a reminder of the unceasing effect of Jesus' Resurrection expressed so memorably by John Masefield in his poem, *Trial of Jesus*, when the centurion answers the questioner at Calvary, "Where is he now?" in words unusual for him, "Let loose into the world, where neither Jew nor Greek can stop him." The Ascension lays its claims upon our interest and devotion and mind, because in it Jesus took finally our humanity which he assumed at the Incarnation, and having redeemed it through his death and Resurrection, he presented it to God as love's highest offering. Only the power of love could do such a wondrous thing. Are you willling to receive that power in order to pass the experience on?

Readying the Twelve for Mission

Easter 7   *Acts 1:14-17, 21-26*

After two such unprecedented events as Resurrection and Ascension, certainly this question is in order: what can God do for an encore? Or, one might simply exclaim: what a hard act to follow! The eleven disciples left Mt. Olivet and returned to Jerusalem, as Jesus had commanded them. Naturally, they sought out the Upper Room, a place filled with memories that were now sacred. Other faithful persons joined them until they numbered about a hundred and twenty, (v. 15) including a number of women with Mary and Jesus' brothers. (v. 14) Here occurred the first congregational meeting of the infant church, with Peter acting as spokesperson for the group.

Did they have an agenda? Well, yes and no. Echoing in their minds were Jesus' words before his Ascension: "Go ... and make disciples of all nations, baptizing them in the name of the Father and of the Son and of the Holy Spirit, teaching them to observe all that I have commanded you: and lo, I am with you always, to the close of the age." (Matthew 28:18, 20 RSV) What an assignment! What a challenge!

Palms and Thorns

But look at their only resources, their meager man-power, in the face of the vested interests of the prevailing Jewish religion and culture, not to mention the vast conglomeration of sects of the Gentile world. Think of it: only eleven disciples, and of these just four or five could be counted on to spearhead Jesus' idea of a world mission!

With our historical hindsight we know now that the period of waiting which Jesus commanded was followed by that great Day of Pentecost when the Holy Spirit descended upon this group and galvanized them into a movement that launched the evangelical movement of the early church. However, our text today (Acts 1:15-17, 21-26) outlines an incident of a somewhat routine nature that occurred between the Ascension and Pentecost. Peter, with more sense than he had generally hitherto shown, stood up and called their attention to an item of unfinished business. This time he didn't put his fishing rod in his mouth. He talked with regret about the defection of their brother, Judas, and he did so in a temperate fashion, concluding with the words, he went "to his own place." (v. 25) St. Chrysostom echoed this thought when he wrote, "No man can hurt a man but himself." The immediate agenda now was to elect someone to take Judas' place. St. Ignatius once said: "Pray as if everything depended upon God" (the group had done this), but he added, "Act as if everything depended on oneself." The group didn't have their heads entirely in the clouds; they got down to business over a concrete detail.

You all know the story. Two names were put forward in a sort of primary (it must have been by a voice vote): Barsabas and Matthias whose qualifications were well known and acceptable to all. Then a season of prayer was decided upon, followed by a casting of lots which put responsibility upon each one to vote as his or her conscience seemed to be led by God. Matthias was chosen, and now the original band of chosen disciples again numbered twelve.

Lent and Easter

What, now, do we make of all this? As this post-Easter season ends, is there a message here for modern church people? Consider these three observations:

1. *It says something to the whole worshiping congregation of the church.* In every congregation there are official members whose names are on the roll titled, "By Profession of Faith." They are eligible to serve on its boards, partake of Holy Communion and represent that congregation before the courts of the denomination. But there are others, numbering in some large centers, in the hundreds, who worship regularly, pay their dues, believe sincerely, but who are nameless and often unrecognized. They constitute a resource which church members often neglect.

Consider Matthias: Peter described him as one who had "accompanied us during all the time the Lord Jesus went in and out among us," all the way from Jesus' Baptism to the Ascension. He was not merely a loose hanger-on; he was a sincere and steady fellow traveler whose integrity commended him to the others; he was really a partner among equals. Indeed, Scripture records many of similar character: In the Book of Ezra we read the account of the dedication of "the house of the Lord in Jerusalem" in which every significant group of names is listed. And then, like an afterthought, we read, "There were among them 200 singing men and singing women." (Ezra 2:65 KJV) No one knows the names of those who thronged the Master on that first Palm Sunday. Little is known about Nicodemus and Joseph of Arimathea, yet they took care of the body of Jesus after his death and laid it in the tomb. Every Sunday in every pew in the local church there are what someone called, "God's nameless great." They have had their spiritual life enriched and deepened as they have accompanied the church membership through the years. There are many Matthiases among them. Probably a simple season of prayer will lead someone to them and give them a well deserved identity in the greater-enterprises of the church.

2. *It singles out an essential qualification for church membership.* Listen to Peter: "One of these men must become with us a witness to his resurrection." (v. 22) Note how he uses the preposition "to" instead of "of." Anyone can be a witness "of" something, but to witness "to" means much, much more. A disciple is not made by a book or by rules or by political strategy. To be a disciple, one must know intimately the person of Christ, must absorb his message, must sense his purpose and must have experienced a total reorientation of his or her life by his redemptive power. When all this happens, then one cannot help becoming a witness to the Risen Lord and being able to say to the world, in the words of Alexander Maclaren:

We are plain men, telling a plain story ... We want you to believe us as honest men, relating what we have seen. We bring it to you as a thing that happened upon this earth which we saw with our own eyes and of which we are the witnesses.[1]

3. *This simple and unobtrusive incident gives a fuller insight into the efficacy of prayer.* People pray daily for many things, usually for strength to cope with life's problems, for release from anxiety and fear, for love and kindheartedness in dealing with difficult people and for God's blessing upon our families and our homes. Prayer, however, had a further dimension for these disciples and followers of Jesus in that Upper Room. They did not say, "We've got a problem. Let's pray about it." The issue arose out of their praying, not the reverse. God knows what the particular need is, and in our deep spiritual communion with him we become sensitive to its reality and are directed to do something about it. Remember that soul-wrenching night in the Garden of Gethsemane when Jesus agonized in prayer over the choice of the Cross. There came the moment when he had prayed the matter

through, and then he arose and said to the disciples, "Arise, let us be going . . . ." (Matthew 26:46 RSV) That is the kind of prayer we must recover, so that as we rise from our knees, the direction is clear and the decision then is ours. And, as we move outward and onward, ours will be the consciousness that God's will is being done.

---

[1] *Expositions of Holy Scripture (The Acts),* Vol. 8 (Grand Rapids: Eerdmans, 1952), p. 33.

www.ingramcontent.com/pod-product-compliance
Lightning Source LLC
Chambersburg PA
CBHW060845050426
42453CB00008B/837